Summer 1940 ...

German bombers target civilian London, England ...

303 Squadron is scrambled—keen to join the fight...

Buckle up—and fast ...

Oxygen mask on—ready to go...

Eight-gunned Hurricanes race for the sky...

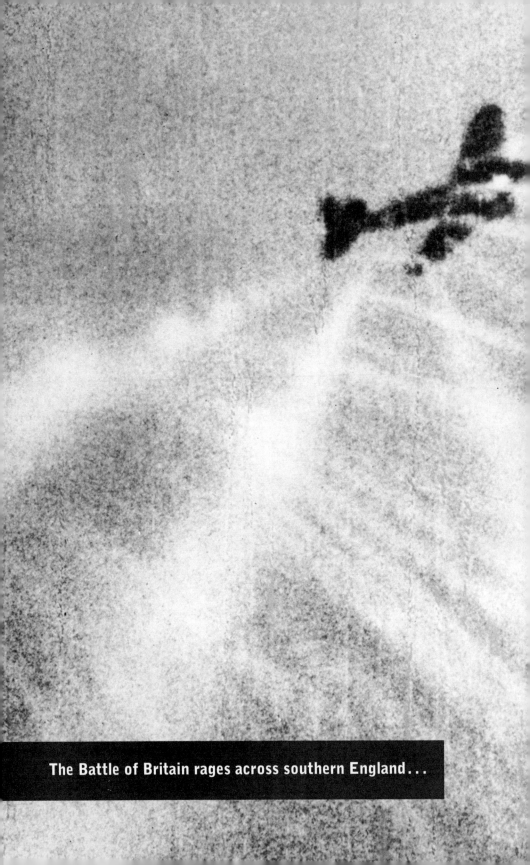

The Battle of Britain rages across southern England...

As Great Britain fights for its life...

AQUILA
POLONICA®

303 SQUADRON

The Legendary Battle of Britain
Fighter Squadron

by *Arkady Fiedler*

Translated by Jarek Garliński

AQUILA POLONICA (U.S.) LTD.

10850 Wilshire Boulevard, Suite 300, Los Angeles, California 90024, U.S.A.

www.AquilaPolonica.com

Copyright © 2010 Aquila Polonica (U.S.) Ltd.
Original Polish-language version Copyright © 1942 Arkady Fiedler

This Aquila Polonica edition first published 2010.

ISBN (Aquila Polonica edition, cloth): 978-1-60772-004-1
28 27 26 25 24   4 5 6 7 8 9 10

ISBN (Aquila Polonica edition, trade paperback): 978-1-60772-005-8
28 27 26 25 24   5 6 7 8 9 10

ISBN (Aquila Polonica edition, ebook): 978-1-60772-026-3

Printed in the U.S.A.

Library of Congress Control Number 2010931248

Acknowledgements:

Cover design, interior book design and maps in this Aquila Polonica edition are by Stefan Mucha, and are reproduced with permission. Photographs and other illustrative material are reproduced with permission, and are from the collections of the following: Stanisław Błasiak; Cedrowski family; Marek Fiedler; Robert Gretzyngier; Tomasz Kopański; Wojtek Matusiak; Stefan Mucha; Paweł Tuliński; Zbigniew Zieliński; the Bundesarchiv (German Federal Archives); The Imperial War Museum; Mirror Pictures; Narodowe Archiwum Cyfrowe (the Polish National Digital Archives); The Polish Institute and Sikorski Museum; Royal Air Force Museum.

The Appendix entitled 'The Song of 303 Squadron' is based on an excerpt from *Jędrusiowa Dola* (Apostolicum 1999) by Zbigniew Zieliński, which was translated and is being used with the author's permission.

 'HAD IT NOT BEEN FOR THE MAGNIFICENT MATERIAL CONTRIBUTED BY THE POLISH SQUADRONS AND THEIR UNSURPASSED GALLANTRY, I HESITATE TO SAY THAT THE OUTCOME OF THE BATTLE WOULD HAVE BEEN THE SAME.'

BRITISH AIR CHIEF MARSHAL SIR HUGH DOWDING

CONTENTS

CONTENTS

HISTORICAL HORIZON

CONTENTS

Europe 1939

INTRODUCTION

The Battle of Britain and 303 Squadron

For two months during the summer of 1940, the fate of the Western world hung in the balance as Great Britain stood alone, desperately battling for its life against Nazi Germany.

Most of Western and Central Europe had already been overrun by the Germans. With its new Blitzkrieg ('Lightning War') tactics, Germany had defeated Poland in September 1939, and then in a rapid sweep between April and June 1940, conquered Denmark, Norway, Luxembourg, the Netherlands, Belgium, and finally France, despite the nearly 400,000 British troops and the additional forces of the smaller Allies including Poland, who were fighting with the French.[1]

Just weeks earlier, between 27 May and 4 June, the British had narrowly averted a disastrous loss of British and Allied troops at the French beaches of Dunkirk with an extraordinary nine-day rescue effort.

On 14 June, the Germans entered Paris unopposed. The following week France surrendered. Those British and Allied troops still fighting in France scrambled to evacuate to England.

---

[1] Previously, between March 1936 and March 1939, Germany had occupied the Rhineland, taken over Austria, and seized control of Czechoslovakia and part of Lithuania. The Germans had effectively neutralised the Soviet Union in August 1939 via the Molotov–Ribbentrop Pact, a non-aggression treaty with secret provisions for division of Eastern Europe. The United States was not yet in the war—it would be another eighteen months before the Japanese attack on Pearl Harbor in December 1941 triggered America's entry into World War II.

The Battle of Britain began less than three weeks later, on about 10 July, with Luftwaffe raids on British shipping in Channel and coastal waters. 'Operation Sea Lion,' the German code name for the invasion of Great Britain, was launched in earnest on about 8 August. Over the next several weeks, massive Luftwaffe bombing raids targeted RAF airfields, London, and other major industrial and population centres. Their goal: destroy British air defence and weaken British resolve—paving the way for invasion by German ground forces.

Again and again, despite severe losses and overwhelming odds, RAF fighter pilots rose to meet the numerically superior Luftwaffe bombers and fighters. With those RAF pilots were Commonwealth pilots, and airmen from allied nations who had escaped to England as France was falling to the Germans. By far the most numerous of these allies were pilots of the Polish Air Force.

Initially Polish pilots were scattered throughout RAF squadrons, but in late July and early August a number of them were posted to two newly formed all-Polish fighter squadrons under joint British and Polish command: 302 Squadron, assigned to 12 Group RAF Fighter Command defending the Midlands and East Anglia; and 303 Squadron, assigned to 11 Group RAF Fighter Command defending south-east England and the vital approaches to London. It was 11 Group which bore the brunt of the Luftwaffe assaults.

The Battle of Britain reached its most critical phase over a two-week period, from the end of August to 15 September. The entire action of Arkady Fiedler's book *303 Squadron* takes place over these critical two weeks, beginning 31 August when 303 Squadron first became operational.

Despite early doubts by British commanders, the Polish pilots of 303 Squadron immediately proved themselves to be among the most superb of fighter pilots, downing three times the average RAF score with one-third the casualties during the Battle of Britain.

The 303 Squadron record is even more remarkable in light of the handicaps that the Poles had to overcome in just the few weeks after the fall of France. They had to learn enough English to understand and respond instantly to operational commands over their radios. They had to reverse their instinctive reflexes in the cockpit: in their prior Polish and French aircraft, to open the throttle the pilot pulled; in British Hurricanes, the pilot pushed. Speed was measured in miles per hour instead of kilometres per hour. Rate of climb was expressed in feet per minute, and altitude, too, was in feet, instead of metres. Fuel came in gallons, not litres; units of pressure also differed.

Arkady Fiedler began writing *303 Squadron* during the Battle of Britain, spending time with the Polish pilots and ground crew of 303 Squadron at their base at Northolt, West London. He wrote the book in Polish under the title *Dywizjon 303*. The first English-language edition was published in Great Britain in 1942 under the title *Squadron 303*.

World War II was still raging across the globe, and Poland was suffering under the most brutal German occupation in all of Europe. A clandestine edition of *Dywizjon 303* was parachuted into German-occupied Poland in 1943. Copies duplicated by the Polish Underground were secretly passed from person to person. This report of the successes of their fighter pilots, fighting in distant lands for freedom, boosted morale enormously in the beleaguered country.

Dywizjon 303 went on to become a classic in Poland. It is mandatory reading for children in grammar school, and has gone through numerous Polish editions. This is the first new

English-language edition since 1942. This story of bravery, determination and aerial skill is as fresh today as when it was originally written—a story of real-life heroes.

Aquila Polonica Publishing

The cover of the secretly printed
Polish Underground edition of *Dywizjon 303*.

A NOTE ABOUT...

This Edition

This is the first English-language edition of *Dywizjon 303* by Arkady Fiedler since 1942, when it was published under the title *Squadron 303*. At the request of Arkady Fiedler's son, Aquila Polonica commissioned a new translation of a later Polish edition of *Dywizjon 303* in order to prepare this new English-language edition. The publishers are proud to have had the opportunity to work with translator Jarek Garliński on this project. Mr. Garliński translated the main body of the book and the Author's Preface, provided certain explanatory footnotes, and prepared the table of equivalent Polish Air Force and RAF ranks included as an appendix.

This edition has been enhanced by supplemental material, including the Introduction, Historical Horizon, appendices, footnotes, maps, historical photographs and other illustrations, none of which (with the exception of a few of the historical photographs) were included in the 1942 English-language edition. The maps of England use current (instead of 1940) county designations in order to better orient today's reader. In preparing the appendices, and in identifying and locating photographs and other material, the publishers were fortunate to have had the co-operation of Peter Devitt, Assistant Curator, RAF Museum London, and two noted experts in the history of the Polish Air Force in World War II, Robert Gretzyngier and Wojtek Matusiak, both of Warsaw, Poland, whose assistance has been invaluable.

A Note About...

Statistics, Ranks, Etc.

There are certain matters on which various published sources and experts differ. Among the most common are statistics and related information, such as number and type of aircraft destroyed, probably destroyed or damaged; identification of aircraft; number of squadrons or aircraft deployed in an engagement.

One source of confusion regarding such statistics can arise from the difference between the reports filed by pilots immediately after combat ('claimed victories') and the final results ultimately determined by higher authorities ('credited victories'). Another source may be incomplete records, or information that was unavailable until an archive or set of records was subsequently opened to researchers.

The ranks of Polish Air Force personnel is another area of frequent confusion. There are a number of possible sources of confusion regarding ranks, including the facts that Polish airmen who served in alliance with the RAF held ranks in both the Polish Air Force and the RAF, which were not always equivalent; that successive agreements between the Polish Air Force and the RAF revised how RAF ranks were assigned; and that there were different dates involved in the Polish Air Force process of promotions (the order date, the announcement date, the effective date and the seniority date), any one of which might have been used by an author.

Throughout the body of this edition, the statistics are those provided by Arkady Fiedler as updated by him in the later Polish edition of *Dywizjon 303*. In preparing the appendices and presenting the ranks of Polish airmen, the publishers have relied upon the knowledge and guidance of their experts.

A Note About...

Language

In this edition of *303 Squadron*, Polish names and words are written in the Polish language which, with its strings of consonants, diacritical marks and that strange 'l with a slash' ('ł'), can appear impenetrable to most native English speakers. Below is a very abbreviated pronunciation guide which may help to demystify the language.

Polish is fairly phonetic in its spelling (i.e., unlike English, the way a Polish word is spelled is usually how it is pronounced); therefore each sound is represented by one letter or a standard combination of letters. The Polish alphabet is similar to, but not exactly the same as, the English alphabet—here are a few of the principal differences:

1) There is no letter 'v' in the Polish alphabet, so Polish uses the letter 'w' for the 'v' sound. When 'w' is the last letter of a word, it is pronounced more like an 'f.'

2) The 'w' sound, in turn, is represented by the Polish letter 'l with a slash' ('ł').

3) There is no letter 'q' in the Polish alphabet, so Polish uses the letter 'k' for the 'q' sound.

4) The Polish 'j' sounds like the 'y' in 'yes.'

5) The Polish 'c' sounds like the 'ts' in 'cats.'

6) The strings of consonants generally break down into standard clusters, each of which represents a certain sound. Some of the major clusters are:
  'ch'—like the 'h' in 'hand'
  'ci'—like the 'ch' in 'cheap'
  'cz'—like 'tch' in 'itch'
  'drz'—like the 'j' in 'just'
  'dz'—like the 'ds' in 'beds'

'dzi'—a softer version of 'dz,' similar to the 'j' in 'jeep'

'rz'—like the 's' in 'pleasure'

'sz'—like the 'sh' in 'show'

7) The diacritical marks under or over certain vowels and consonants change their pronunciation; for example, 'ę' is pronounced like 'en' as in 'ten' or as 'em' before certain consonants; 'ó' like 'oo' as in 'moon'; the 'ć' as a soft 'tch.'

The accent on Polish words of more than one syllable is usually on the penultimate, or next to last, syllable.

So, for example, 'Warszawa' (the Polish word for 'Warsaw') is pronounced: Var-SHA-va. People who live in Warsaw are called 'Varsovians' in English—derived from the Latin word for Warsaw, 'Varsovia,' and perhaps from the pronunciation of the Polish 'Warszawa.'

This is how the names of some of the 303 Squadron pilots would be pronounced:

Witold Urbanowicz—VEE-told oor-ba-NO-veetch

Witold Łokuciewski—VEE-told wo-koo-CHYEV-skee

Ludwik Paszkiewicz—LOOD-veek pash-kee-EH-veetch

Zdzisław Krasnodębski—ZDZEE-swaf kras-no-DEM-skee

And 'Kościuszko' would be pronounced 'kosh-TYUSH-ko.'

Aquila Polonica Publishing

TRANSLATOR'S NOTE

The original 1942 edition of *Dywizjon 303* was translated under the title *Squadron 303*. In preparing this translation, I have chosen to follow RAF, rather than Polish, military practice in calling this new version *303 Squadron*. For the English reader this is, I believe, more authentic.

One of my principal goals was to be faithful to the tone of the 1940s in which the book was first written. Hence, for instance, I have written 'the skies over England,' rather than 'English airspace,' which would be the modern terminology.

I have left the Polish airmen their Polish military rank rather than using their RAF rank; as an example, I have not translated the Polish 'Porucznik' as 'Flying Officer,' except when it applies to someone other than a Pole. More information about Polish and British air force ranks during World War II when the Polish Air Force was serving alongside the RAF, including the equivalents between the two systems of ranks, is included in Appendix 2.

Finally, at the risk of irritating those who already know their stuff, I have taken the liberty of, from time to time, explaining in footnotes one or two of the allusions which might not be common knowledge for today's reader.

JAREK GARLIŃSKI

3 3
SQUADRON

THE LEGENDARY BATTLE OF BRITAIN
FIGHTER SQUADRON

From the left: Author Arkady Fiedler and Witold Urbanowicz,
Polish OC 303 Squadron.

Arkady Fiedler's military identity card.

AUTHOR'S PREFACE[1]

When in September 1940 I reported in London to the Head of the Polish Armed Forces in Great Britain, General Władysław Sikorski, I was astonished that none of the numerous Polish men of letters in the British Isles had hitherto hit on the idea of chronicling the extraordinary achievements of the Polish airmen of 303 Squadron, which the British press had been extolling to the high heavens.

General Sikorski enthusiastically ordered me to write a broader account of 303 Squadron's actions and directed me to RAF Northolt outside London where 303 Squadron was based. Easily establishing a friendly rapport with most of the squadron, the fighter pilots as well as the ground crews, I eagerly got down to writing what I had decided would be a broader battlefield report, written in the heat of the moment and with a patriot's true enthusiasm: a report, and not a work of literature, since that was what that exceptional time clearly needed.

Among all my books, *303 Squadron* is probably the one truly written 'live,' under the direct influence of the events of 1940: the first pages emerged during the final phase of that extraordinary drama called the Battle of Britain, and I put the finishing touches to the last ones a dozen or so weeks later when, rather like an echo of the battle, the roar of the Luftwaffe could still be heard at night over London and bombs continued to fall on the city.

---

[1] Excerpted from the Author's Preface to a Polish edition of *Dywizjon 303* that was published in the early 1970s.

Although the book was born out of high emotion and although the world has moved on a great deal since then—and the author's understanding has of course matured over the course of these thirty-odd years—I must with some surprise record the fact that while preparing the book for a new edition, I did not need to make any major changes to it. The parts that I have somewhat altered deal with minor, incidental and secondary matters.

303 Squadron, as a picture of the heroism of the Polish airman, gained a wide audience and effectively achieved its goal. It aroused sympathy and recognition for the Poles among readers in Great Britain and the Dominions, in the United States, in French-speaking Canada and in Brazil, and went through several editions. Proof of the eagerness with which it was read in these countries are the almost three hundred press reviews, most of them positive.

In 1943, the book appeared in Occupied Poland. A miniature edition produced in London was parachuted into Poland by air, and there were several subsequent underground printings within Occupied Poland. In that especially grim year for Poles living under a reign of terror, this book played an extremely important role in providing a boost of much-needed encouragement. It stiffened resolve and infused many with new courage— possibly the greatest satisfaction and reward a writer can have. The publisher of the English version of *303 Squadron* took advantage of the book's success in Occupied Poland by including on the 1945 dust jacket a blurb to the effect that it was 'the only Polish book, written in exile, but also published in Occupied Poland in 1943.'

ARKADY FIEDLER

POZNAŃ, POLAND, JANUARY 1973

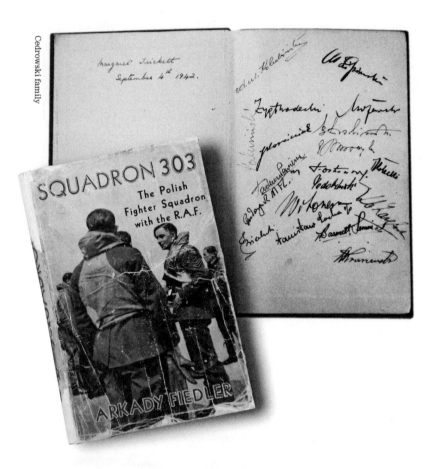

A 1942 edition of *Squadron 303* signed by pilots and other personnel in the squadron. The book was a gift from Tadeusz Cedrowski, a fitter in 303 Squadron, to his English girlfriend Margaret Trickett.

On 11th October 1940, 303 Squadron was moved to RAF Leconfield for R and R.

303 SQUADRON COMBAT AREA
31ST AUGUST TO 15TH SEPTEMBER 1940

CHAPTER 1

The Battle of Britain 1940

ALL OF us saw it, all of us lived through it, and yet we clearly need to remind ourselves of it once again: the summer of 1940 was horrific. It was a dreadful time for all people of goodwill. That July no birds sang for them, no sun could warm them, not for them even the simple pleasure of sharing daily bread with their loved ones.

The whole free world rubbed frightened eyes to dissolve a nightmare, but awoke to a reality even more dire. The world was shaken with hitherto unknown convulsions, the hearts of billions of people trembled from the worst premonitions, from anxiety, despair, doubt. Everyone, from the highest to the lowest, sensitive souls and more ponderous ones, the cockney from the Thames, the native from Brazil, the miner in Pennsylvania, the rancher in Australia and the planter in Java, everyone watched as if transfixed. All hope was lost. They lived in anticipation of eventual defeat—the defeat not only of Great Britain, the last free bastion of Western Europe, but of the whole civilised world.

Their desperation was not the result of enemy propaganda

1

or fifth column[1] influence. They had another source for their fears: facts. Bare facts. The cold iron logic of facts.

And these are the facts they faced:

After only a week of fighting, the might of Nazi Germany had dealt Poland, known as a valiant warrior, a mortal blow, and after four weeks had completely trampled and prostrated her. In a similarly short time, it had crushed and subjugated wealthy France, another Ally and one with the reputation of having the finest soldiers. Along the way, it had swiftly destroyed five smaller nations. It had managed to inflict two defeats on Great Britain, the last remaining Ally: a painful reverse in Norway, and a crushing blow in Belgium. Fortunately for Britain, these were defeats on foreign soil.

Now, everything pointed to a final battle on the final field: the British Isles themselves. Given what had happened, how much hope remained?

The situation was grim indeed. Winston Churchill had bluntly said so to the British people. With brutal honesty, he cautioned his nation on the likelihood of invasion, and vowed that, if necessary, in a final desperate effort British citizens would defend every beach, every house, every street, every pasture.

The German preparations took six weeks following the Fall of France in June. On the 8th of August 1940 the offensive began,[2] 'the final act of this drama of war, which would,' so the

---

[1] The term 'fifth column' refers to a group of people who clandestinely work to undermine a larger group from within, usually to the benefit of an external enemy. It was used in Poland at the beginning of World War II to describe Poles of German descent who helped the German invaders, and was also widely used in Great Britain to refer to German spy rings operating within the country. Translator's note.

[2] The 8th of August 1940 is frequently cited as the official beginning of 'Operation Sea Lion,' the German code name for the invasion of Britain. During the prior month, beginning around the 10th of July, the Luftwaffe had focused on attacking British shipping in the English Channel. Translator's note.

insolent tyrant Hitler boasted, 'see the British Empire scattered to the winds by autumn.'

The Germans brought in no new weapons for this offensive. They attacked England with a well-tried method: the Luftwaffe, their air force. This terrifying spearhead, using the fury of bombs by the thousand to sow destruction, had carved out a path for the German ground forces to achieve victory in all their campaigns to date, in Poland, Norway, Holland, Belgium, Denmark, Luxembourg, France. There, the Luftwaffe had been decisive. It was now expected to be no less decisive in Great Britain.

Starting on the 8th of August, swarms of German war-birds massed over England. The first day there were 300 of them, a few days later 600. The Battle of Britain exploded into life.

This battle, which was to last for a full two months, was one of the most extraordinary in the history of man, and also one of the most momentous. One of the most extraordinary, because it was conducted entirely in the air—a few hundred British fighter pilots defending against thousands of German bombers and fighters.

One of the most momentous, because the stakes were so high. If the Germans succeeded in controlling the skies over-head, then England would be at their complete mercy. Destruction of principal British centres of life would be only a matter of time and number of bombs. Defence against actual invasion would become virtually impossible. But first the Luftwaffe had to control the skies. Over the two months of the Battle of Britain, the Germans launched ninety-eight major attacks using approximately 6,000 aircraft.

Wave after wave of German planes stormed the skies over England with uninterrupted violence. The hordes of aircraft hurling destruction attacked from the south and the east.

Repulsed and scattered, they would return like so many heads of the Hydra transformed into wings bearing the black cross.

The Luftwaffe's initial objective had been to paralyse British shipping in the English Channel, and destroy the ports and coastal airfields. It did not destroy them; it paralysed nothing. The gates for the invasion were not opened: in the way stood the Allied fighter pilots.

During the battle's second phase, the German High Command wanted to throttle the RAF in its nest by destroying the airfields that protected London. It failed. Allied fighter planes retained command of the skies. In the battle's third and final phase in September, London itself, its existence and Britain's heart, now became the target. London survived; Britain's heart was not ripped out.

The middle of September saw the climax of the Germans' pressure. The invasion of England was scheduled to be launched between the 15th and 20th of the month. Preparing the way, the Luftwaffe unleashed its fiercest attacks, relentlessly hurling brimstone and fire to terrorise and finally crush the British. On the 15th, the Germans launched two decisive major offensives. Each contained more than 250 bombers and fighters representing over 400,000 combined horsepower and a corresponding weight of firepower and bombs. At that moment England was defended by 250 fighter aircraft armed with 2,000 heavy machine guns. The British defended, and they won. The wreckage of 185 German aircraft, over a third of the total, was scattered over the fields of Surrey, Sussex and Kent; an equal number of damaged German planes limped home; the rest, having accomplished nothing, fled.

The German aerial armada was defeated. There was no invasion.

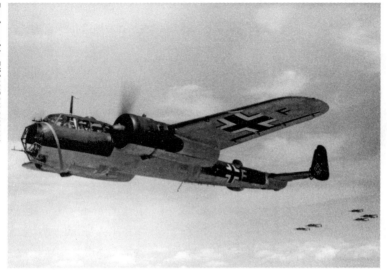

Swarms of German bombers gather over France...

...and skim across the English Channel on their way to bomb England.

RAF Hurricanes take to the skies as
the Battle of Britain explodes into life.

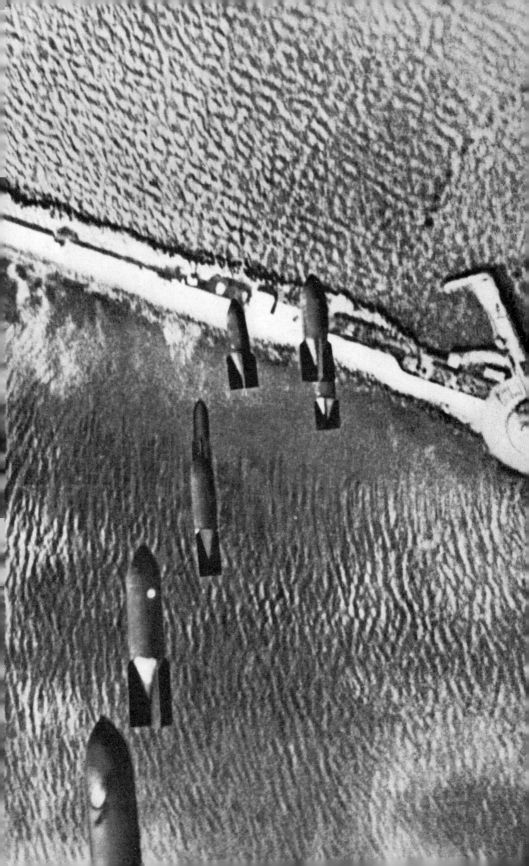

Preceding page: A stream of German bombs
hurtles towards a harbour installation.

A 303 Squadron Hurricane destroyed during the Luftwaffe bombing of RAF
Northolt on the 6th of October 1940. Antoni Siudak, a 303 Squadron pilot,
was killed on the ground during the same bombing raid.

Photographed from a German bomber, an RAF Sptifire flies below a Luftwaffe
Dornier bomber during a dogfight.

Pilots of 303 Squadron.

Mechanics of 303 Squadron, with one of the squadron mascot dogs.

One hundred and twenty-six victories—the official score of 303 'Kościuszko' Squadron in the Battle of Britain, making it the highest scoring RAF squadron during the battle.

303 Squadron roll of honour in Officers' Mess at RAF Northolt. A portrait of Tadeusz Kościuszko hangs at the top, with photographs of those killed or missing displayed in rows below. The airmen killed have a black diagonal stripe across the right corner of their portraits.

Victory in the Battle of Britain not only saved the British Empire. It broke an evil spell for humanity—people now realised that the Germans could be beaten. They were not invincible, and their weapons, though powerful, were not omnipotent. In July 1940, the Luftwaffe was still a spectre haunting the whole world. Two months later, the devil's charm had dissolved: the sun began to shine again for people of good-will, their daily bread regained its flavour.

This was achieved by a handful of Allied fighter pilots— wonderful, young, oh so young men, real and unflinching heroes. They were modest men, smiling, healthy and strong. The Luftwaffe threw into the fray its excellent and best equip-ment, and its finest airmen. However, the British Hurricanes and Spitfires turned out to be even better machines, and the Allied fighter pilots champions over the German aces.

Already after the battle's first phase, Winston Churchill accorded the British pilots the highest accolade. Speaking bluntly, he uttered the memorable words: 'Never in the field of human conflict was so much owed by so many to so few.'

Indeed, there were few of them, but what they accomplished equalled, in the opinion of some chroniclers, the Battle of the Marne in the First World War.

This valiant band included Polish fighter pilots alongside the British. The famous 303 'Kościuszko' Squadron, stationed at RAF Northolt near London and composed almost entirely of Polish fighter pilots, joined the Battle of Britain in its final decisive phase. 303 Squadron was in combat for forty-three days of the Battle, from the 30th of August[3] to the 11th of October 1940. This squadron, with a glorious and long tradition, had been named in honour of the group of gallant American fighter pilots, known as the Kościuszko Squadron, who had flown with the fledging Polish Air Force in the 1919–1920 Polish–Bolshevik War. Now, true to the Kościuszko emblem, 303 Squadron astonished the world with its valour, courageously fighting shoulder to shoulder with its British colleagues in defence of English soil.

Altogether, in the course of the Battle of Britain, 303 Squadron shot down a total of 126 German aircraft, of which the Polish pilots' haul was 93, its three British pilots' was 16, and its one Czech pilot's was 17. The squadron took part in more than a dozen major engagements, and in several it clearly played a decisive role.

In just one month, the critical month of September 1940, 303 Squadron shot down 108 out of the 967 enemy aircraft destroyed by the entire RAF with all its Allied pilots, in other words about 11 percent. In a friendly rivalry with its Allied comrades, 303 Squadron then held the record for 'kills' among all the fighter squadrons defending Great Britain, while the next highest-scoring squadron, a British one, had only 48 kills, in other words, less than half.

The Polish squadron bought this victory with the death of five of its pilots, a loss which was disproportionately low, indeed two-thirds lower than British losses that month.

The 15th of September was to become the anniversary for the RAF of the Battle of Britain. It would also become an

---

[3] 303 Squadron entered combat even before it was officially operational, when Lieutenant Ludwik Paszkiewicz broke away from a training exercise on the 30th of August to shoot down a Messerschmitt 110, initially claimed as a Dornier 215. Translator's note.

anniversary for the Polish fighter pilots serving in England, since it was on that day they distinguished themselves by their valour and success. This joint anniversary will surely become a mainstay for all time of Polish–British amity.[4]

---

[4] Sadly, these words, reflecting the feelings of the majority of Polish airmen in Britain during 1940 and 1941, did not come true. Certainly, the 15th of September became an important anniversary for the RAF, but the Polish airmen were brutally and unceremoniously cast into oblivion.

In the first post-war years the RAF celebrated the 15th of September every year, and all newspapers and magazines in Great Britain expatiated at length about the Battle of Britain of 1940—but for the most part nothing was said about the Poles. If they were mentioned at all, the coverage was embarrassingly meagre, monosyllabic, or even clearly skewed, as in, for instance, the edition of the otherwise serious journal *The Sphere* from the 25th of September 1948: in an article entitled 'Recollections of the Battle of Britain' there was not a word about the contribution of Polish fighter pilots to the Battle of Britain. The article did mention 303 Squadron in glowing terms, but it completely omitted to say that it was composed mainly of Poles, whereas—in an act of supreme perversity—all that it said of them was that one of the Polish pilots had written a story called 'The Cloud,' which the author of the article personally felt to be one of the best novellas of the war. I am gratified that that contributor to *The Sphere* had read my book *Squadron 303* and honours one of its chapters with such a mention (he even calls me a pilot), but it would have been more honest of him if he had not in the meantime forgotten about the real heroes of those days: the Polish fighter pilots. Author's note.

Chapter 2

The Fighter Pilot

THE KNIGHT among the wonderful race of pilots is the fighter pilot, the airman *sans pareil*: his sworn duty to protect. To protect his bombers from the enemy who attacks smiting from the air; and to protect his own land from the enemy bombers who seek to destroy it. Sometimes, the fighter pilot uses the firepower of his machine guns to attack an enemy on the ground, but this he does infrequently. His effort, his victories, his dramas for the most part are played out above the clouds, high in the sky, where the view is greatest, heaven nearer, and the earth below blurred and distant, like a dull dream.

The fighter pilot protects, but he does not fight behind a passive shield. Quite the contrary, protecting, he hurls himself at the enemy with all the momentum of the thousand horses harnessed in his engine. The fighter pilot always attacks, always assaults. He always goes in, to use an analogy from another area of warfare, with his bayonet fixed.

This herd of a thousand horses carries him like a fury and allows him to charge at a speed of 450 to 600 feet per second. For people walking safely on the ground it is difficult to imagine what this means and just what changes this can make to a human being. The fighter pilot—on the ground as normal as the next man—in the air becomes someone else, a demon of speed. He has lived for perhaps a quarter century at ground level, and has been training for several years to act decisively in the air within seconds. Death approaches like lightning, and only lightning reactions can avert it. Help, if a split-second late, may mean defeat. The great air battles over England in September 1940, which sometimes swept across several counties, never lasted longer than ten or fifteen minutes. Often during these few minutes the outcome of the war or the fate of the Empire hung in the balance.

On the ground the fighter pilot lives like other men: he loves, drinks and laughs. Like others, he knows why he hunts his enemy and why he must be relentless in his hunt. But when the aircraft leaves the ground, all the pilot's earthbound emotions fall away: complex feelings of love or hatred remain behind. Aloft, there are only the simplest survival instinct and a feel for the great game. He is a complex instrument panel and his only objective is an enemy aircraft.

The idea of the Polish fighter pilot supposedly recalling the great wrong done Poland as he squeezes the trigger is something that well-intentioned people on the ground have imagined. A fighter pilot may indeed recall this great wrong, but before combat, or later, after it is all over. During actual combat things happen so quickly that the pilot is unable to distinguish details, and later when he thinks back, his mind is a blank; he experiences a sort of mental blackout.

In the air a new biological process takes over, one so fantastic that only the great imagination of a Leonardo da Vinci could have foreseen it. The straps securing the fighter pilot to his machine before take-off are a telling symbol. In the small cockpit the pilot is unable to move; he is locked inside his plane like a brain inside a skull. Indeed, he is a brain in the skull of a metallic bird.

As he ascends, a remarkable change takes place. The man grows into the machine; they fuse into a single living organism: a new creature, half man, half machine. The more sensitive fighter pilots clearly feel that their nerve ends reach to the tips of their aircraft's wings. They feel them physically and emotionally. If an enemy damages one of their wings, they feel the shock as if they had been wounded themselves.

The engine is the enormous heart of the fighter pilot, who is seemingly now without a heart of his own. His life is linked to this great heart and if it ceases to function, then disaster ensues.

In the air the most important sense is sight. Spotting the enemy, reacting instantly, aiming flawlessly, and hitting the target—all depend on perfect vision. Many fighter pilots have experienced the odd sensation that their eyes are growing, becoming stronger and eventually encompassing the whole man, who to all intents and purposes ceases to exist and becomes one great big eye. There is nothing odd about this: the giant eye must not only serve the man, but the whole giant machine. It must be large and effective.

The organic union between man and machine is most clearly seen at the moment of firing. This is the culminating moment for which the fighter pilot exists, his raison d'être. Almost all fighter pilots agree that when aiming and firing, every part of their body is involved, not just their eye and their thumb on the trigger. They explain this sensation by the way in which a fighter aircraft is constructed: the guns are on fixed mountings in the wings, so the pilot directs fire at his adversary using himself and the whole aircraft.

A Polish 'knight of the air.'

303 Squadron was not equipped with Spitfires until shortly after the end of the Battle of Britain. This 303 Squadron Spitfire IIA P8041 RF-E was photographed in early 1941.

303 Squadron pilots discuss tactics.

The rounds, pouring out of both wings in a visible stream, become like claws. They pierce the enemy and tear at his body. They are a living tool of the will to win. The tension is sometimes so overwhelming that the fighter pilot feels the nerves of his arms extend into the rounds, as if he were tearing at the enemy with his own hands.

The Polish fighter pilots' marvellous victories in September 1940 were a real eye-opener for the rest of the world. A great many people tried to discover their secret. There were several, of which three seem to be the most important: superior eyesight, superior Polish tactics, and superior determination.

The Poles usually had better eyesight than their British colleagues. This appeared to be a specific attribute of the Polish airmen—the vision of a hawk which allowed them to see further and more sharply. This was allied to great powers of observation, akin to an inborn instinct to focus, thanks to which they were able to sum up a situation faster and more accurately than the British.

The Polish fighter pilots' tactics hinged on not messing about too long with their adversary. They liked to seize the first possible moment and strike like the wind, to get in as close as possible, almost to touch the enemy, then let him have a full, murderous, eight-machine-gun blast from a distance of only a few dozen yards. Outside experts initially criticized such close-range tactics as unnecessary, madcap bravado—until they realised that the 'madcaps' were getting more kills and, strange to tell, were suffering far fewer losses.

Within every Polish airman burned more or less the daring streak of a Cossack horseman, of an hussar, of an uhlan.[1]

---

[1] Light cavalryman. Translator's note.

This quality evidently comes in handy even three miles above the ground, where the Poles successfully carried out cavalry charges, on the backs not of a single horse, but a thousand. Breaking up the whole enormous German bomber armada on the 15th of September 1940 was no less of an heroic achievement than the charge at Somosierra,[2] but it had a more profound moral impact and brought the Poles more honest glory than did that Spanish affair.

The third reason for the Poles' success was their grim determination. Read an account of the Polish nation's suffering since September 1939, and you will understand the determination of a Polish fighter pilot.

---

[2] A famous charge by Polish cavalry in the Peninsular War in 1808. Translator's note.

CHAPTER 3

31st August: The First Battle

31ST AUGUST 1940, 18:00 hrs. 303 Squadron is in the air, patrolling the London area. This is its final day of flight training. The next day the squadron will finally appear on the operational map and join the Battle of Britain, which has been raging in the air for three weeks. For three weeks the Polish pilots have been waiting impatiently, eager to get into the fight.

In an immense blue sky, the angled rays of the red late-afternoon sun wash the ground in gold and, from a height of 20,000 feet, England looks like a dreamland of tranquillity and happiness. Beautiful, England in August! The Polish fighter pilots are under its spell...and they dream of combat.

The squadron is under the command of Squadron Leader Ronald Kellett, an Englishman. Short, a little overweight, with an apparently jolly face, Kellett was a splendid fighter pilot who had shot down seven Germans in France. But today, he is a commander in trouble. He is worried, unsure of the Polish pilots' abilities in combat. He does not know them! He has been their English OC, sharing command with a Polish OC, for only a few weeks. He will command them in their first dogfights over England the next day. Will the Poles be up to the task?

They have supposedly seen action in Poland and France. To be sure, they are fine fellows. But at the same time Kellett is surprised and troubled that these foreign and unknown fighter pilots from the depths of Europe have been entrusted—doubtlessly due to exaggerated Allied courtesy—with one of the most vital locations, where their task will be to defend not only a critical sector of the air battle, but much more: the British capital and heart of the Empire—London. Is this not carrying inter-Allied courtesy just a little too far?

London spreads below and to one side like a mighty, grey stain. Even in the brightest sunlight there is always a haze of smoke and mist over the city. Barrage balloons, pink in the sunlight, poke their plump bodies out of the murk. On this day Kellett has no eyes for the charm of the English countryside; he looks down at London and worries. About tomorrow and the days to come...

18:12 hrs. Suddenly a voice crackles through the headphones. An order from ground control: '303 Squadron, A Flight, come to heading zero nine zero!'

What is this? A new, unexpected manoeuvre? Six aircraft peel off from the squadron and, under Squadron Leader Kellett's command, head east along the designated vector.

Ground control again: 'Heading one zero zero.'

Sounds odd, like the start of a decent adventure. The five Polish fighter pilots feel a rush of excitement. Could this be it?...

Then a sharp order: 'Heading one four zero!'

No doubt about it. Ground control is vectoring them. Onto an enemy?

Yes, the enemy! A few minutes' flying time, and the fighter pilots see them, far away, slightly to port. A group of bombers, clearly visible. They are heading for France, probably having accomplished their mission, or at least having seen combat; some of the aircraft are trailing smoke. Above, as always, and a little to the rear, an escort of more than a dozen Messerschmitts, German fighters, is flying in a loose formation.

Without hesitation, the Polish flight attacks. The Poles have a favourable position, flying out of the sun. They accelerate. The idea is to cut across the bombers' path at an angle before the Germans leave England. The fighter pilots burn with enthusiasm. At last! At last they would sink their teeth into the enemy.

They sink their teeth in, but not quite as they had imagined. They never reach the bombers. They are still a good two miles away, when suddenly a section of Messerschmitts appears, barely 500 yards away and right in front of the Polish flight. Three stragglers from the German formation. By a strange coincidence they have not spotted the Poles. The Germans are coming up in a wide turn, the Poles below them are hidden by the Messerschmitts' wings and also dead in line with the blinding sun.

Squadron Leader Kellett's section hits them swiftly from behind. Kellett and his two wingmen, Sergeants Eugeniusz Szaposznikow and Stanisław Karubin, get on the Germans' tails, each choosing his man. Taken by surprise, the Germans do not see it coming. Kellett is the first to open fire. At a range of a hundred yards and in the blink of an eye, he sets the middle Messerschmitt ablaze, giving the Polish flight a fine show. The German aircraft explodes and drops to earth, trailing a tail of fire like a comet.

The other two Messerschmitts now dive, saving themselves with a lightning turn. But the Polish sergeants leap at them with no less lightning speed. They dive too, clinging to the enemy like pincers. They will not let go. Szaposznikow is in superb position—diving almost straight down, he instantly calculates the exact angle and carefully aims below his adversary's fuselage, forcing the Messerschmitt to fly through a hail of rounds. The intense burst seems to rip the guts out of a living body. They are deadly rounds.

Karubin meanwhile dives, maintaining position above the third Messerschmitt. He holds his fire. He waits. He watches. When finally the German begins to pull out of his dive, Karubin drops on him like a vulture. At close range, he fires three quick bursts into the engine and the rear of the cockpit. The enemy, streaming thick smoke, crashes to the ground.

The destruction of the three Messerschmitts lasted only seconds, less time than it takes to tell. But during these seconds another drama was unfolding behind the victorious trio, and Squadron Leader Kellett had no idea that his own life hung by a thread.

For, at the very moment when Kellett's section was attacking the Germans, three other Messerschmitts suddenly appeared from behind, flying to their comrades' rescue. They opened fire at long range to drive off the attackers. They missed. It was in any case too late; the first three Messerschmitts were already doomed.

In their haste, the rescuers had committed a cardinal error: they had failed to take into account the two Polish fighters covering the rear of the flight. The Messerschmitts flashed past the Poles as if they did not exist, a blur of black crosses rushing into battle.

With full boost from their superchargers, the Poles, Second Lieutenant Mirosław Ferić and Sergeant Kazimierz Wünsche, wingmen for the second section, charged off in pursuit. This mad dash formed a complicated pattern: first

Squadron Leader Kellett, British OC 303 Squadron.

From the left: Ferić, Grzeszczak, Zumbach, Henneberg and Kent.

Witold Żyborski, 303 Squadron adjutant and 'papa.'

From the left: Brzezowski, Wójtowicz and Szaposznikow, with a Hurricane in the background.

From the left: Wünsche, Karubin and Szaposznikow.

came the three Messerschmitts already on fire, then came Squadron Leader Kellett's section, then the three other Messerschmitts, followed by the two Poles.

The German rescuers were almost within effective range of Kellett and Szaposznikow when the two Polish fighters caught up with them. Ferić took the starboard wingman and Wünsche the port one. Both opened fire at almost the same instant, with an almost identical result: the two Messerschmitts, mortally wounded, plummeted, one gushing billows of black smoke, the other a blazing mass of flames. The third Messerschmitt, which had not been attacked, bolted for safety.

Total victory! Five burning Messerschmitts plunged to the ground. Like flaming comets, they portended ill for the enemy. A real massacre. Two of the pilots managed to come down on their parachutes; the others perished in the flames and the wreckage. A victory all the more remarkable because it had happened so smoothly and rapidly, effortlessly. It was team-work of the highest class, clean combat.

And it was intoxicating. The Polish fighter pilots were electrified. These Hurricanes! What a revelation! An unrivalled tool in the hands of a fine pilot, with eight machine guns that provided an incredible and crushing weight of fire.

All the fighter pilots but one had found success in this engagement. The sixth one, Lieutenant Zdzisław Henneberg, who had been leading the second section, had his own victorious adventure a few moments later. Seeing the defeat of the first trio of Messerschmitts and unaware that his wingmen had already gone into action behind him against the second group, he waggled his wings indicating that they should follow him. He flew off to where he had spotted four more Messerschmitts. They were about 2,000 yards away and seemed oddly jumpy. All four were making defensive manoeuvres. Henneberg easily caught up with them. Only then did he discover that he was alone, without any support.

He did not back off. Come what may, he had decided to bag his 'little Adolf'[1] too. A seasoned hand, he did not rush blindly into a suicidal attack. He took up a suitable position, a few hundred yards above and behind the Messerschmitts. Thus he followed, biding his time, mile after mile, like a wolf stealthily pursuing a flock.

They crossed most of Kent and were approaching the Channel. Dover was off to the side. The Messerschmitts, even though numerically superior, showed no signs of wanting to fight. They seemed rather to be fleeing in panic. After a while, there was confusion among them, and one drifted several hundred yards away from the rest.

This is Henneberg's moment. He dives at full throttle into the gap. Before the Messerschmitt can get back to his comrades, Henneberg hits him at an angle with two quick bursts. The black cross turns sharply and dives. Henneberg stays on him. Two more quick bursts. The Messerschmitt begins to smoke. They are now over the coast. Another burst. The Messerschmitt is dropping like a stone. Suddenly a huge fountain of water, and then a long white streak beneath the surface, like a gigantic torpedo. The streak settles, deeper and deeper, then it sinks, blending with the surrounding sea water. The Messerschmitt has disappeared completely.

Scenes of indescribable glee at the airfield. The pilots, the ground crews, indeed everyone now knew or had guessed the

---

[1] A colloquial term used by the Polish pilots to signify a German. Translator's note.

news. They all appeared outdoors as the Hurricanes returned one by one, each doing the fighter pilot's customary victory roll before landing. Enthusiasm was boundless.

After the fifth Hurricane, there was a gap. Ten minutes went by, a quarter of an hour. The sixth plane was missing. Anxiety! In vain, all eyes scanned the sky. The most worried of all was Captain Witold Żyborski, the squadron adjutant, a doting 'papa' and the whole outfit's father figure.

Then a tiny dot appears in the sky. It grows. Here comes the sixth one! Lieutenant Henneberg, alive and well. He had done as well as the others: he had bagged a sixth Messerschmitt. So as he did his sweeping roll above his comrades' heads, a surreptitious tear welled in 'Papa's' eyes. A tear of joy and pride. And a feeling that the Polish squadron's great days of achievement and glory were just beginning.

The British have a fine sense of fairness. If truth be told, Squadron Leader Kellett was not really comfortable with the Poles. But at that moment, overcome by a strange emotion, he began to shake his pilots' hands. He had to admit, not without some slight jealousy, that these were fighter pilots of the highest class. They could fight as a disciplined team, but they also knew how to pluck a victim with impudent panache right from the hornets' nest.

'I am delighted,' the British Air Marshal commanding the RAF cabled the Poles that same day.

A few days later, after fresh successes, an astonished and delighted Britain echoed his sentiments, and a fortnight later— it was the whole world.

303 Squadron had entered the Battle of Britain in a blaze of victory.

CHAPTER 4

2nd September: Comradeship

DOVER, A bridgehead on the British Isles, was an exceptionally significant spot. Here both land and air were vital. Plump barrage balloons bobbed in the sky like a flock of grazing sheep. Funny and unwieldy, yet dangerous and menacing: some airborne daredevil could get tangled in their tethers and crash to his death. For the British, they were innocent little lambs; for the Germans, a thorn in the flesh. So the Germans hated these balloons and stubbornly attacked them.

It was the 2nd of September. A whole squadron of Messerschmitts was approaching from the south-west, from the direction of Hastings. Hiding in scattered clouds, the Germans crept like burglars along the coast to Dover. They wanted to take the town by surprise. But before they could even think of diving at the balloons, they were themselves surprised: British fighters materialised in front of them. The fighters of 303 Squadron.

Dover had never seen a better show than the dogfight that now broke out. More than twenty aircraft circled, looped, rolled and arced, using every aerobatic stunt, yet this crazy confusion was so strikingly graceful that to spectators on the ground it looked more like a dance, or some grand mediaeval pageantry, than the reality of total war.

The Messerschmitts did not last long. Although no-one had yet been shot down, the Poles in their more manoeuvrable Hurricanes were clearly gaining the upper hand, sitting on their opponents' tails with ease. One by one the Messerschmitts, pressed too hard, began to dive and pull away from the mêlée, haring over the Channel for France. Gradually the sky over Dover emptied, until only a fantastically intertwined mass of white contrails remained, long, slender tails of the fleeing aircraft. The chase now sped out over the Channel. The Messerschmitts fled like startled deer, furiously hunted by the Hurricanes.

The Polish squadron had accomplished its mission, chasing the enemy from Dover.

One of the pursuers was Second Lieutenant Ferić. Two days earlier he had had a marvellously easy victory, and he had made up his mind that today he would help himself to another 'little Adolf.'

The Messerschmitt he had chosen clearly knew what was coming. The German was twisting restlessly, weaving unnecessarily, and seemed to be losing his nerve. This allowed Ferić, after hitting top speed, to draw within reasonable range. At 300 yards he punched out several bursts.

The reaction was so unexpected that Ferić was dumbfounded: the Messerschmitt banked and did a perfect barrel roll, then continued to fly in a straight line. This idiotic and theatrical manoeuvre was of no help to the German at all.

'Greenhorn!' thought Ferić, and decided to finish him off as quickly as possible.

There was no time to lose. Down below, the coast of France with its ferocious anti-aircraft batteries was already visible.

As a result of the roll, the Messerschmitt had lost a further hundred yards in the race. Ferić watched him with pleasure through his sights: the fuselage loomed large in the middle of the red circle like a wild grey dove, and as helpless as a dove.

Ferić's second burst hit the Messerschmitt plumb in the middle. The Messerschmitt dived sharply, Ferić right behind. But suddenly, to his dismay, something dreadful happened. Everything went dark; his cockpit was covered by a mysterious veil. Fluid spurted from his engine and poured over his windscreen. By the liquid's greenish colour Ferić immediately recognised oil. His hair stood on end: the oil lines had ruptured.

The Polish pilot of course instantly gave up the chase, pulled out of his dive, and turned back for England. He could not finish off his enemy, but he was no longer thinking of that—it was now a matter of saving his own life. He opened his canopy, used a handkerchief to wipe the windscreen. It helped a little.

Then another shock. Thick clouds of smoke started to billow from the exhaust pipes. His Hurricane might burst into flame at any moment. Ferić unstrapped himself, the easier to be able to leap out. He waited, anxiously gazing down at the sea below, which appeared a grim sheet of lead. No pilot likes the sea, but now to Ferić it looked like the jaws of hell.

Fire had not broken out, but something just as catastrophic was happening: without a flow of oil the engine had seized up. The Hurricane was beginning to vibrate violently, as if riding over cobblestones. Hastily Ferić cut off the fuel

Ferić

Daszewski

Paszkiewicz (*on the left*) talking to Walters, the squadron interpreter.

Witold 'Tolo' Łokuciewski (*foreground*) wearing his flying suit.

supply. The engine stopped. The aircraft, relying now on its aerodynamic qualities alone, went into a glide. This was his last chance.

He was at an altitude of about 20,000 feet, and the English coast was fifteen miles away. Would he make it? The aircraft was now nothing but a heavy mass of metal, dropping slowly, helplessly, and responsive only to one force, the malevolent whim of gravity. Could he glide all the way to safety?

But that was the least of his worries. Ferić was gripped by another, more powerful anxiety: he was quite defenceless. It was the 2nd of September, the Battle of Britain was raging over England. Scores of Messerschmitts would be returning this way. Ferić, poking along as slowly as a tortoise and with a smoking aircraft, was clearly visible for miles. The clumsiest novice pilot could crush him as easily as a sparrow in a cage.

His heart was in his mouth; he felt like a man whose arms and legs had been broken. Ferić was no longer a proud fighter pilot, ready to take on the whole world, but a miserable insect on whom anyone could tread. He was a soldier without a weapon.

Well, they had spotted him! He could see to one side through his streaked windscreen that an aircraft was heading his way. It was 500 yards off, now 300, now it should be opening fire. Ferić glared at the plane as if he could drive it off by sight alone.

But the other man did not shoot. In fact, quite the contrary, it was a comrade, Second Lieutenant Witold 'Tolo' Łokuciewski. He had seen the Hurricane's plight in the distance and had come to its rescue. He had recognised Ferić. With a wave, he indicated that he would stay close by and guard him.

A moment later another Hurricane joined them, also one

of theirs from 303 Squadron, Lieutenant Ludwik Paszkiewicz, who had broken off his pursuit of the enemy as soon as he had seen the unusual procession. Now Ferić had two friends alongside.

They covered him. They knew that they risked greater danger in the event of an attack by a more numerous enemy, since they would not flee. But they had no qualms whatsoever. They were prepared to die in defence of their comrade: they would stay.

Ferić relaxed. The worst had passed, and he could now calmly look after his aircraft. The clouds of smoke had fortunately disappeared. The pilot concentrated fully on his flying, trying to get the maximum lift out of his wings for the glide. All three Poles had the same concern: would Ferić make it to England, or would he crash into the sea?

They had now passed the middle of the Channel. England was becoming clearer, although the coast approached terribly slowly. Ferić anxiously gazed again and again at the altimeter. The needle dropped relentlessly, with a terrible, cruel patience. The soulless instrument seemed to be passing judgment: 9,000 feet, 7,500, 7,200...

It was then that the escort fighters noticed two aircraft far ahead, flying towards them, heading for France. They were off to the side and much higher. The Poles immediately recognised the shape: two Messerschmitt 109s. The Germans had spotted them, too. Clearly intrigued by the slow-moving group and scenting an easy kill, the Messerschmitts turned and flew towards the Polish trio.

Paszkiewicz and Łokuciewski prepared for battle. They climbed and began to circle watchfully high above Ferić.

The Messerschmitts came around to sit on the trio's tails and, with the advantage of greater altitude, followed behind.

For a moment they hesitated. Then they circled the Poles again and took up a position for attack, getting right into the sun.

The two Polish fighters, ceaselessly circling over Ferić, did not let the Messerschmitts out of their sight. Their calm circling expressed a firm resolve. The rings that they drew around their comrade seemed to have magic powers. The Germans began to realise that before they could get their hands on their defenceless prey, they would have to face some vicious talons.

The Messerschmitts hesitated again. They came nearer still, to 500 yards, but they kept postponing their attack. Watching closely, they appeared to be seeking a weak point in the defence. Seconds passed, weighty as an age. The Germans waited too long. Their moment had passed; their nerve had failed them.

They gave it up. Suddenly they turned and flew off towards France.

The altimeter was merciless: 5,500 feet, 4,500, 4,200… Still four miles to go, three miles…The English coast was becoming clearer. 4,000 feet, 3,000… A thrilling race between two rivals: distance and height. Which would win? The sea was coming ever closer, now Ferić could see individual waves—but he could also see little houses on land. A few minutes more, and the wings seemed to be winning the race. Yes, they were. The wings were winning, those good, honest and faithful wings.

The aircraft crossed the coast at a height of 1,000 feet. The wings had won! They had saved a life. The fighter pilots sighed with relief, and a warm feeling of gratitude filled their hearts. They could not remain silent. Regulations be hanged!

'Hello, hello!' called Ferić somewhat hoarsely into his microphone and when his comrades replied, he said emotionally: 'Thank you!'

But the others took refuge in jests and laughter. Łokuciewski replied: 'You must be kidding! Is the whisky on you tonight?'

'Maybe even a couple!'

'Not enough; make it three!'

And while they were doing their whisky trade, Ferić was looking for a place to make a crash landing.

Down below in the misty uncertainties of earth, matters of life and death are a complex, tormenting, often insoluble enigma. But at the height of 20,000 feet, the problems of life, death and duty are simple and clearly solved—just as the sunlight is brighter there than at ground level.

Life, death and duty are three steely, unbreakable forces. And yet sometimes out of them springs a tender, precious flower: comradeship. It is a flower both precious and unusual, for once it has grown, it can withstand the harshest winds and endure the heaviest storms for many a long year.

CHAPTER 5

When the Ammunition Ran Out...

DETERMINATION IS as lethal a weapon as a gun. The more determined soldier always wins. He wins because his will is more powerful, his stamina stronger, his eye keener, and so his rounds more often find their target.

This war saw no fighter pilots more determined than the Poles.

Now here was little Sergeant Stanisław Karubin, merely a boy. He looked no more than twenty and was little older. He had a round face quick to break into a smile—but his eyes were proud, smouldering, aggressive, black.

That day he was up with 303 Squadron, chasing a pack of enemy bombers over the Thames Estuary. Others caught up with the enemy, but Karubin did not, for a dozen or so German fighters attacked his section on the way. Karubin twisted down and got away, but lost contact with the rest of his squadron.

Diving down, a solitary Messerschmitt came into his sights. He fired at once, but missed. Now it was a duel. Violent manoeuvres, circling, flips, and Karubin, thanks to his greater agility, got on the German's tail. The Pole punched out a long burst. A kill! The Messerschmitt began to fall, trailing a large plume of smoke.

The young Pole had conducted the quick dogfight in cold blood, without emotion, almost without thought. Not like a man of blood and nerves, but like a machine of steel. An efficient, superb tool honed for battle in an excellent school.

Blood and nerves, the man in him, and blind rage, came to life only a moment later. Karubin was still looking with satisfaction at his enemy's death throes—the finest sight for a fighter pilot—when like a bolt of lightning out of a clear sky, a stream of rounds flashed a treacherous track over his head. A new adversary! The unexpected attack roused the victor from his daydream. And although Karubin escaped the danger with a sharp turn, he was trembling with fear and anger.

'Bloody hell!' he snarled like an angry dog as a Messerschmitt streaked past him, plummeting downward. Behind it, some way back, chased two Hurricanes. Karubin, without further thought, instantly dived and followed them.

They dropped right down almost to the river, flying at tree-top height. First the Messerschmitt, then the two Hurricanes, and then Karubin. They passed the white houses of Gravesend, bleached by sea winds and rain; they flew low, like fearsome gulls, past real gulls, past green meadows and grey sails—hundreds of sails and fishing boats.

They passed one of the most enchanted corners of England: the Thames Estuary. The London haze, turning the afternoon sun pink and yellow, creates here, where land and water meet, a strange trick of the light, a delicate picture of exquisite colouring. The magic of this light and the rich beauty of the boats has charmed British painters for generations. They come here as if to their own sanctuary. Even the great Turner had found inspiration for his paintings in these parts.

Karubin (*right*) with a mechanic standing in front of a Hurricane.

Ground crew rearm and refuel the Hurricane RF-E while Karubin climbs into the cockpit (he is visible behind the mechanic standing on the wing).

Messerschmitt 109 marked with the distinctive Balkenkreuz (the black cross) used by the German Luftwaffe during World War II.

That day the roar of four engines, like a shriek from the depths of hell, shattered the riverside peace and deafened every living thing on the water. It was a poignant symbol of the times, its composition especially telling: a German, two Britons and a Pole. Violating the eternal spirit of the Thames, these four fighter aircraft were but a small cog in the ghastly machine, the machine of war that was shaking the world to its foundations and engulfing every nation in its workings. Yet now its significance could be reduced to one simple question: whether the light and mists of the Thames Estuary were to remain an inspiration to British genius...

The fleeing Messerschmitt left the river, turning to starboard, crossing broad meadows, cutting south-east across Kent, taking the shortest route to France. Karubin did not like the way this was going. The 'little Adolf' was setting a good pace and might easily get away. The two Hurricanes seemed unable to catch him; they were barely able to keep up with him.

Karubin put on full boost. His machine roared and leapt forward, as if lashed by a whip. The Pole felt the joy of a horseman who spurs his steed into a wild gallop. Suddenly light-hearted, he hummed the old Polish cavalry song:

How glorious it is when an uhlan
Rides in the midst of a war...

Racing at top speed, he quickly passed the two Hurricanes. Near Rochester he began to close on the Messerschmitt. Now only 500 yards behind. Still hugging the tree tops, so close to the ground. The black cross grew with every second. Karubin felt a soldier's affection for his machine: a miracle, not a machine! Like riding a hundred lightning bolts!

Now only 300 yards. Karubin quickly glanced down at the trigger of his machine guns. The safety was off. Without pressing the button, he ran his thumb over it delicately, tenderly. Yet this thumb was also the claw of a predator. He was almost in position... the German was holding a steady course. An easy target! But the Pole did not fire just yet. Closer, he must get closer! He had time...the German would not get away! ... 150 yards, 100, 70...

Right! Karubin disengaged his supercharger. He took aim and fired. From dead astern, right through the Messerschmitt's tail...Hell! His shots had no effect! The enemy was still showing him his heels.

Karubin, hot on the scent, changed course slightly. He fired another burst at an angle into the German's side, where he was most vulnerable. That did it! He had hit a vital artery. A thin stream of smoke came from the Messerschmitt—like a thin stream of blood from a wounded animal.

But wait... it was not a vital artery! The Messerschmitt did not burst into flame, the thin stream of smoke had stopped. His enemy still tore ahead at full speed. Karubin clenched his jaw. He closed in; he was now right on the Messerschmitt's tail. He took aim—and the next moment was almost killed.

Focused on his sights, Karubin did not see that the Messerschmitt was flying straight at a tree. The German at the last minute hopped over it, while the Pole almost flew into it. Violently he pulled up. Branches scraped the bottom of his fuselage, but luckily caused no damage. The Hurricane sped on, unharmed. Karubin was drenched in sweat.

'Damn the bugger!' he swore at his wily opponent.

At murderous range, perhaps fifty yards behind the Messerschmitt, Karubin opened fire a third time. Imagine his astonishment and sore disappointment, almost to the point of pain, when, after only a dozen or so rounds, his guns fell pitifully silent. Out of ammunition! His adversary flew on. Rotten luck! The Pole at once realised that it was not surprising—after all, this was the second opponent he had taken on that day.

Karubin turned aside to let the other two Hurricanes finish the job. But a quick glance showed that they would never catch the Messerschmitt. Too far behind.

Down below a town appeared. Grey cathedral walls: it had to be Canterbury. Canterbury already! Barely three or four minutes to the sea. Meanwhile the Messerschmitt was surging ahead at full speed. Nothing to stop him, no-one to block his path.

Karubin was seized with despair and a sudden, uncontrollable hatred. His eyes glared, terrible, inhuman eyes. He had a score to settle with this enemy, not only a soldier's score, but an even worse one: a human score. He had to destroy this German at any cost! Any cost!

He raced flat out again. He swung even further to one side, and overtook his prey. Then, in a sudden desperate rush, Karubin turned and charged—a crazed torpedo of rage—right at the Messerschmitt as if to ram him.

He did not ram him. He flew just over his enemy's aircraft. Three feet—maybe less!—above the German's cockpit canopy. For a fraction of a second Karubin saw the pilot's upturned face, contorted in deathly terror—then he had flashed past.

Behind him, he heard the dull roar of a mighty crash.

The German had not been able to stand the strain. His nerve had given way. His hand had twitched on the joystick. That twitch was all it took.

Gaining height, Karubin circled back. He returned to the spot where the Messerschmitt had ploughed into the ground.

A huge cloud of dust and smoke. Tongues of flame flickering amidst the scattered wreckage. One wing lay fifty yards from the crash; the remains of the other, a hundred yards away. Of his enemy, nothing remained but a heap of wreckage and a dark cloud of dust.

Karubin circled overhead. He drank in the scene of destruction. His eyes were back to normal: proud, smouldering, aggressive. He, a little Polish sergeant, had also drawn inspiration from the Thames Estuary, his own personal, special war-time inspiration...

Yes, this war saw no fighter pilots more determined than the Poles.

Their oh so understandable zeal to fight the German foe had already given birth to a great many legends, picked up by the world's press, in which the fanatical warrior, after using up his ammunition, hurled his aircraft at his enemy's, and of course paid for the victory with his life.

Truth is stranger and more beautiful than fiction. The Polish fighter pilot, after using up his ammunition, indeed hurled himself at his enemy—but only one of them died: the enemy.

CHAPTER 6

5th–6th September:
You Win Some, You Lose Some

THE BATTLE of Britain raged on. Day after day German bombers invaded the skies over England. They battered away at the British bastion, attempting to smash and destroy it. The Germans were astonished: the bastion continued to hold out. The Germans were furious: the bastion continued to fight.

During the third week of the Battle, the Germans recognised that they did not yet control the skies over England. So, changing tactics, they focused all their aerial resources, the whole might of the Luftwaffe, on a single target: Fighter Command. It had to be pulled up by the roots, once and for all. For two long weeks—at the end of August and the beginning of September—German bombers vented their fury on RAF airfields, while German fighters tried to sweep their British rivals from the sky.

The British stood their ground. The Germans, drunk with arrogance, had already announced to the world that they had crushed England, broken its resistance. Yet day after day British squadrons, uncrushed, unbroken, audacious and endlessly valiant, would rise to meet the invaders and, parrying their thrusts, would wound them, inflicting three times as many casualties as they suffered themselves. The Germans waged an obstinate, superhuman struggle using brute force. Yet every day the waves of attackers broke against hard British granite. The Germans had not realised just how hard that granite would be.

During that period, 303 Squadron won a glorious victory. On the 5th of September, out of an overall total of thirty-nine German aircraft shot down that day, 303 Squadron bagged eight, 20 percent of the total, with the loss of only one aircraft whose wounded pilot survived.

At this point, the Polish fighter pilots' frequent successes raised doubts in the mind of RAF Northolt's Station Commander, Group Captain Stanley Vincent. He suspected the Poles of fiddling their numbers, exaggerating their victories in their reports.

Vincent, wanting to see things for himself, took to the sky on the 5th of September. Flying alongside 303 Squadron, he was in luck. He was a delighted eyewitness to the Polish fighter pilots' daring and to their 'devilish effectiveness.' With nine Hurricanes, which was all they could muster that day, 303 Squadron broke up a sortie of Junkers, shooting down three bombers; and when at that moment a swarm of Messerschmitts arrived in support, 303 Squadron quickly dispersed them, destroying four in the process. All the Poles returned alive, having lost only a single Hurricane.

There was more. Vincent also saw one of the Poles, Sergeant Wünsche, save Squadron Leader Kellett. Kellett was in serious trouble—a Messerschmitt had him in his sights, but before the German had time to fire, Wünsche, spotting the situation, raced to Kellett's aid and 'shredded' the German.

303 Squadron OC
Major Zdzisław Krasnodębski

A spider's web of contrails.

Miropix

Hurricane RF-E taxiing at RAF Northolt.

A Hurricane is carefully checked for damage by the ground crew before its next sortie.

'Good heavens!' exclaimed Vincent, when he landed at RAF Northolt. 'They really are doing it! They are wonderful madmen!'

The following day, the 6th of September, was obviously scheduled by the Germans as the Day of Judgment for British Fighter Command. From early morning the Luftwaffe swarmed overhead in greater numbers than ever before, using a new tactic which was extremely dangerous for the defending fighter pilots. Not only did the German fighters escort their bombers, but they also independently patrolled the whole sky in small groups, thus creating a living bridge from the Channel coast deep into the heart of England.

'The sky looked like an aquarium with a great many little fish in it!' later remarked one of the fighter pilots who fought that day.

303 Squadron took off at 08:45 hrs., once again with only nine aircraft. Ground control, as always, gave a heading: south-east. At the half-way point between London and the coast, the pilots saw a disturbing sight: countless Messerschmitt patrols. They were flying very high in pairs, at an altitude unattainable by the Hurricanes. Some of the Germans were circling over one spot, others, tracing larger figures, swept in great spirals northward into the depths of England. At that height they were quite invisible from the ground, but their white contrails betrayed their presence. The crystalline sky was patterned with more and more contrails, until at last it looked as if an invisible spider were weaving a giant, sinister web over the whole country. And it was a deadly spider that was preparing this web.

Despite the threat from the superior numbers of enemy aircraft overhead, 303 Squadron held the required heading. Everyone was on full alert, vigilantly watching the sky, straining to see above and behind. The squadron was on an awkward course, straight into the blinding sun. It was difficult to see anything ahead. A milky, foggy glow spread before them, a dazzling flicker of sunlight, a curtain of hidden secrets and unpleasant surprises.

A group of enemy bombers burst out of the glare, heading in the direction of London and passing the Poles some 2,000 yards to starboard. Behind them flew a screen of Messerschmitts, which were just being attacked by a squadron of Spitfires. A magnificent opportunity for 303 Squadron! Without hesitation, the squadron leader decided to attack. Banking sharply to starboard, he tore after the bombers at full throttle. The squadron followed.

They did not get far.

A swarm of Messerschmitts fell on them. Like a pack of frenzied hounds, the Germans attacked from the front, the rear, the sides. With a threefold advantage—altitude, speed and the sun, to which was added a fourth: overwhelmingly greater numbers—the Messerschmitts pounced upon the nine Hurricanes. The assault was devastating. With the first burst, the Hurricane of the Squadron OC, Major Zdzisław Krasnodębski, was hit. Krasnodębski, one of the finest Polish fighter pilots, baled out, badly burned.

A fighter pilot's skill is displayed not only in the offensive, but also in the defensive role. Above all, in the defensive role. While every soldier is easily able to take cover from enemy fire, a fighter pilot at an altitude of 20,000 feet has nothing but empty sky around him. Only lightning manoeuvres and exceptional, superhuman presence of mind, can save him.

The Messerschmitts' sudden attack under such favourable conditions should have wiped out all nine Hurricanes with the first blow. It destroyed only one. The others escaped the

Krasnodębski tries to sleep
between German raids.

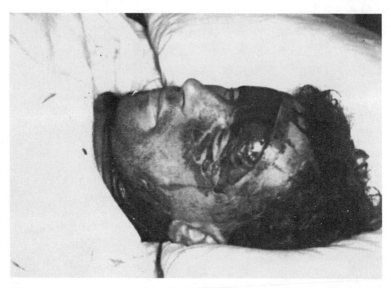

The badly burned face of Krasnodębski. Burns were a constant fear of pilots.

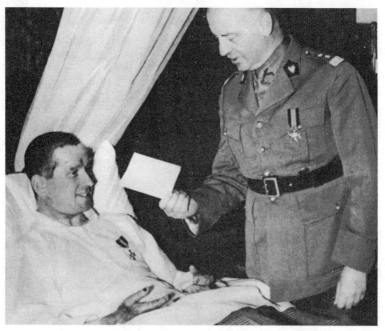

While still in hospital recovering from burn injuries, Krasnodębski is awarded the Virtuti Militari by General Sikorski.

ambush with spine-wrenching manoeuvres, and in a moment the enemy had lost the advantage of surprise. German rounds hit only empty space. Now the battle flared into individual dog-fights, an indescribable chaos of air combat. 303 Squadron bared its fangs and unsheathed its claws. It would not be swept aside so easily!

Seeing a Messerschmitt's yellow nose heading straight for him, Lieutenant Witold Urbanowicz, who had recently joined the squadron from 145 Squadron, a British unit, instinctively hauled on the joystick. His Hurricane banked so steeply that he almost blacked out. Painfully he realised that at this moment of weakness his enemy would shoot him down. But the German did not. After recovering consciousness, Urbanowicz saw the Messerschmitt ahead of him, diving. He flung himself after the German. They circled each other. Once, then again. Closer, more aggressively. The third time around, Urbanowicz got on the German's tail, firing at a range of sixty yards: the first burning Messerschmitt tumbled out of the battle.

Meanwhile, Sergeant Stanisław Karubin, little, deter-mined Karubin, was mopping up another Messerschmitt when he saw below him three Heinkel bombers. He dived straight at them, spraying a hail of rounds. The starboard Heinkel went down in flames—but at that same moment, Karubin was hit by fire from one of the bombers. Wounded in the foot and thigh, with his instruments shattered, the side of his cockpit torn off and a wing damaged, Karubin nevertheless managed to twist out of range. The forlorn invalid landed somewhere on the fields of southern Kent in one piece. But before he was knocked out of the fight, he had given those Germans their money's worth.

Sergeant Wünsche rushed to help a Spitfire, which was flying straight on apparently unaware that a Messerschmitt was on its tail peppering it with rounds as if at target practice. Wünsche closed up on the German who, after two bursts from the Pole, spiralled downwards, smoking. But Wünsche was a moment too late: the Spitfire was also spiralling downwards, and its pilot was clambering from his cockpit to bale out.

Meanwhile more Messerschmitts were swooping in from all parts of the sky, like hungry jackals scenting easy prey. They all headed straight for the same spot. Eventually there were over a hundred of them—so many, that in the pandemonium of battle they kept getting in each other's way. The Hurricanes and Spitfires which remained were unable to engage normally. Forced into purely defensive manoeuvres, wriggling desperately like hunted eels, they escaped from one German only to be attacked by another, hit by a burst here, a burst there... but even in such desperate straits, they did not lose heart.

Now Second Lieutenant Ferić, himself pursued, suddenly saw a careless Messerschmitt in his sights—a perfect target. A long burst: the black crosses erupted in flames. In the ensuing mayhem, Ferić dived like a falling stone and got away. Athol Forbes, a British flight lieutenant from 303 Squadron, was not so lucky. He also bagged a Messerschmitt, but was himself shot up and had to bale out.

The high point of the battle passed, the drama was ending. The final Hurricanes and Spitfires slipped out of the trap. Only the Messerschmitts remained, but they too, exhausted by the battle, headed back to France on their last gallons of fuel. The sky emptied, the roar died away. Silence returned to the hills of the Weald and the Vale of Kent. On the ground smouldered the wreckage of more than a dozen aircraft. A few parachutes, like giant mushrooms, were still dropping lazily from the sky.

That day 303 Squadron suffered severe losses. Five out of its nine Hurricanes were destroyed. Four pilots were wounded, one was killed. However, the squadron had shot down seven German planes. But that was not its real victory. Its achievement was that, on a day when the Germans believed that they would deliver a final coup de grâce to Fighter Command, the Polish squadron, by standing firm and defending furiously, had drawn upon itself the greater part of the German attack and had blunted it. 303 Squadron, together with a Spitfire squadron, had played the part of an aerial Winkelried.[1] Once again, the German plans were foiled.

The formation of German bombers which had escaped the Poles continued on its way, but with a weakened fighter screen. It did not reach its objective. Further inland, Fighter Command launched other fighter squadrons into the attack, and easily smashed the German assault.

The last of the parachutists touched earth. Overhead, only white contrails remained from the ferocious battle...but they too slowly melted away in the azure sky. The menacing spider web collapsed, the symbol of the deadly spider vanished.

Once again, for now, the sky over England was at peace.

That same day 303 Squadron received the following letter from General Władysław Sikorski, Polish Prime Minister and Commander-in-Chief:

London, 6 September 1940

Allow me to pass on to 303 Squadron 'congratulations on a fine day's work.' These greetings were

---

[1] Arnold Winkelried was a Swiss hero who is supposed to have sacrificed himself in the Battle of Sempach against the Austrians in 1386 for the good of the cause. The character was known to Poles from Juliusz Słowacki's play *Kordian*. Translator's note.

sent to me by the Minister of Aviation, Mr.
Archibald Sinclair. In addition to the words of
His Majesty King George VI sent to the President
of the Republic, this is the second public recognition of the Polish airmen's exceptional combat
qualities. Having recently valiantly joined the fray
alongside their famous British colleagues, they
can this day take pride in their major success.
Their achievements are the only honourable
response a Pole can give to the disreputable lies of
German propaganda.

Supreme Commander
Sikorski

These congratulations and recognition from the highest
British sources reflected the eager enthusiasm which the
whole of Great Britain felt for the Polish fighter pilots who
were so successfully defending British territory. But they also
had a deeper, more political objective: raising Britain's morale
by demonstrating that it was not alone in this mortal battle
with the Germans, that its Polish allies believed in Great
Britain's eventual victory. In those desperate days for the
British, even such a source of encouragement played an important part.

Thus one could see the 6th of September 1940 and the two
succeeding weeks as the period of maximum goodwill towards
the Poles in Great Britain.

During those fevered days of battle for Fighter Command,
when violent combat raged over England day after day, the
position of Polish commander of 303 Squadron, left vacant

after Major Krasnodębski had been shot down, needed to be filled immediately. Air Vice-Marshal Keith Park, AOC No. 11 Group, did not hesitate: he knew his pilots well and he knew whom to trust. He appointed Lieutenant Witold Urbanowicz, hitherto Krasnodębski's second-in-command, as OC 303 Squadron. The following days would show how good a choice this was: Urbanowicz distinguished himself as a commander, and also became an ace of aces, a true slayer of dragons, as the Battle of Britain hurtled frantically on and the determined enemy kept coming.

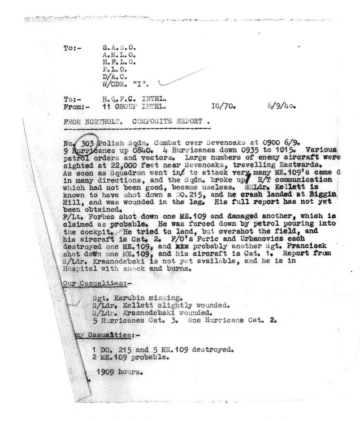

RAF intelligence combat report that records Krasnodębski's injuries.

CHAPTER 7

7th September:

A Tasty Morsel—Dorniers

THE 7TH of September was warm, clear and fine. Sunlight bathed the land. The day had been quiet. Only in the afternoon, at 16:32 hrs., did the blow fall: German bombers got through to London.

It was a Saturday. As usual, the city was blissfully enjoying its weekend. In the East End poor folk relaxed in the slums, children played in the streets, thousands of people watched sports matches or were at the dog track.

At 16:30 hrs., small white bouquets blossomed in the sky on the south-east horizon: explosions of anti-aircraft shells. These little posies raced closer, closer, swift as the wind. Air raid sirens began to wail, the barrage of gunfire grew louder, the roar of dozens of aircraft filled the air, and suddenly a stream of death and disaster poured from the sky. High explosive and incendiary bombs fell like hail, raining down on warehouses, homes, women, children, fuel tanks, gardens, the docks, dog tracks, gasworks—bombs rained and rained, seemingly without end. They continued to rain down as if they were going to wipe the East End of London off the face of the earth.

Docklands east of London are hit by German bombers.

Residential London is set ablaze during 'The Blitz.'

Ludgate Hill, in the City of London—life goes on.

Fuel tanks exploded, the docks flamed to the sky, warehouses blazed, people perished.

Without doubt, the airmen of the black crosses enjoyed the spectacle of this hell they were creating, laughing even with devilish glee. They were exhilarated that finally they had been able to strike a bloody blow right into the proud heart of the despised British Empire, in broad daylight, blatantly and with impunity. They were buoyed too by a victor's arrogant certainty that Fighter Command had ceased to exist. For if it did exist, would it have allowed them to reach London so easily?

Indeed, the German bombers, about forty of them, flew in a tight formation of threes, while above them a similar number of Messerschmitt 109s flew top cover. It is no secret that this was a black day for London and a black day for Fighter Command's senior officers. They had failed to intercept the attack.

303 Squadron was scrambled late, only a few minutes before London was hit, and was immediately despatched to the north of the city where it was vectored onto a south-easterly heading over the Thames, heading for the docks. The pilots could already see in the distance the telltale smoke from anti-aircraft batteries. A moment later, in front of them and to starboard, a formation of Luftwaffe bombers appeared. The bombers were flying below 303 Squadron, but their Messerschmitt escort was flying high above it. The bombers, approaching the Thames from the south, dropped their bombs on its banks and headed north across the river.

The Polish pilots believed that Flight Lieutenant Forbes, leading them that day as British OC, would at once bring the squadron around for a ferocious attack straight at the enemy to prevent the bombing of the docks, if that was still possible. But this did not happen. Forbes, not having a clear view of the enemy's flight, missed his chance. He maintained the same course, flying right past the head of the bomber formation about 2,000 yards away. Continuing to hold the same course, 303 Squadron began to draw away from the German formation. It was a critical moment. A few more seconds on this heading, and the squadron would irretrievably lose the opportunity to attack.

Lieutenant Paszkiewicz, commanding the second section, seized the initiative. He was a fighter pilot of long experience, an exemplary airman and an energetic warrior. Waggling his wings as a sign to the other aircraft, Paszkiewicz broke formation with his section, simultaneously banked to starboard and dived. The German bombers were several hundred yards below and now almost behind the squadron. Lieutenants Henneberg and Urbanowicz charged after him with the third and fourth sections; they all banked and dived as he had. The first section, commanded by Forbes, quickly noticed its colleagues' manoeuvres. They now turned, following the others to take up the rear.

While 303 Squadron was thus swinging around in a great arc to advance on the German bombers, high overhead another drama was taking place, one which was extremely important and beneficial to the Poles' operation. A few seconds earlier another Hurricane squadron had swooped down and fiercely attacked the bombers' fighter cover. It had immediately engaged most of the Messerschmitts, thus depriving the bombers of effective fighter protection.

The bombers, Dornier 215s, were flying in close formation in groups of three, forming a dense mass to provide a better combined defence. In theory, this flying castle represented considerable firepower: about 120 machine guns. But when

From the left:
Zumbach
and Daszewski

Dornier bombers crossing France.

303 Squadron Hurricanes at RAF Northolt.

From the left: Urbanowicz in the foreground. Standing: Walters, Forbes, Łokuciewski, Paszkiewicz and Group Captain Pawlikowski.

faced with a single fighter squadron of daredevil acrobats, deadly masters of attack, this whole group of bombers was as clumsy and defenceless as a tortoise on its back.

An aerial bloodbath followed. Point-blank bursts of fire cut through the Dorniers in a massacre like few others in the annals of air combat. Paszkiewicz's section was the first to attack, targeting the rear bombers. Urbanowicz's section drilled into the enemy's starboard flank. Henneberg's did the same on the port flank. Forbes's section hit the leading ranks. They took the enemy from all sides. Twelve angry hornets with murderous stings. Twelve raging hounds ripping into the carcase of a wild boar.

They tore that carcase to pieces.

The first Dornier immediately burst into flames under Paszkiewicz's fire. Sergeant Szaposznikow picked off another Dornier to port. Sergeant Stefan Wójtowicz got a third to starboard. A fourth bomber, attacked by Second Lieutenant Łokuciewski, 'burst like a bubble.' Second Lieutenant Jan Zumbach 'scythed' a fifth one out of the sky. Two fighters from the first section, Forbes and Second Lieutenant Jan Daszewski, chopped down two Dorniers. Meanwhile Urbanowicz had been setting another bomber ablaze. Paszkiewicz took down his second kill, as Wójtowicz was also getting his second one.

This all happened incredibly quickly, efficiently, almost gracefully. Sportingly. The Dorniers fell out of the sky like partridges, sometimes a brace at a time.

The attack was so rapid, that only at this stage were unengaged Messerschmitts coming down to help. They arrived too late. The bombers had been routed, the formation shattered. The remaining Dorniers were heading for France at full tilt, singly, in pairs, stealthily, any way they could. Retreating in confusion and panic, flying blind. No longer were the

German airmen sniggering. Gone were their arrogant smiles. The enemy who had set fire to the London suburbs was now perishing in the flames of his own aircraft. The remnants fleeing over East Anglia were caught and destroyed by other Hurricanes and Spitfires.

Some of the pilots of 303 Squadron turned to tackle the Messerschmitts. Henneberg shot down a Messerschmitt 109, Szaposznikow another, Lieutenant Marian Pisarek a third. Pisarek's luck ran out on this one. His Hurricane was shot up and he had to bale out. As he started to jump, his left shoe caught on the edge of the cockpit—for some time he flew with the aircraft, hanging head down. At last he managed to pull his foot out of the shoe. He landed safely in his sock, but he was embarrassed. The sock had a hole in it.

Zumbach was the last one in the squadron to shoot down a bomber, his second of the day. Fleeing in panic, a Dornier blinded with fear flew across Zumbach's line of fire at a range of twenty yards. After a burst, such a stream of flame erupted from the German that the fighter pilot, fearful for his own aircraft, banked like lightning. He blacked out and only recovered 12,000 feet below, not far above the burning suburbs. He came to just in time.

In this one battle 303 Squadron had fourteen confirmed kills and four probables. Its own losses: two aircraft, one pilot wounded...and one shoe. That day other RAF squadrons shot down sixty-one aircraft and lost twenty of their own. The anti-aircraft batteries also did a fine job, destroying twenty-eight aircraft: their best score of the war.

Spotting a new wave of German bombers, Urbanowicz hurriedly landed at the first airfield he saw east of London for more fuel and ammunition. He found the airfield deserted. He taxied from one end to the other. Nothing.

Black clouds of smoke rose over the burning suburbs, darkening half the sky. From that airfield the situation looked serious, as if the whole of London was in flames. Somewhere nearby anti-aircraft guns continued to hammer, sending up a curtain of fire. A little further off, the distant thud of bombs exploding. The battle continued to rage all around.

At that moment a British corporal appeared and politely invited Urbanowicz into a bomb shelter. There the fighter pilot found a few other soldiers, the crew of a nearby machine gun position. It was just five o'clock, teatime. The men were calmly drinking tea, smoking and quietly chatting. It didn't matter what was going on around them; after all, it was teatime.

'How about a nice cup of tea?' the friendly corporal asked and, not waiting for an answer, served his guest.

A bomb fell nearby, creating a shock wave even in the shelter.

'My, my!' The corporal smiled, and continued calmly to spread jam on his bread.

Urbanowicz could not stand it. His nerves were still strained: less than fifteen minutes before he had been surrounded by masses of murderous Germans, flying and fighting like hell. This calm tea ritual seemed to him a crazy daydream. He shouted at the corporal to take him, at once, immediately! to an ammunition and refuelling crew. The corporal stared at him in amazement, but did as he was bidden. This crew was also drinking tea in a bomb shelter, but the men gave Urbanowicz what he needed. As he took off, he felt that he was waking from a nightmare.

Back in his own element, Urbanowicz felt better. His anger

passed and he grew more cheerful. But the words 'a nice cup of tea, a nice cup of tea' kept buzzing in his ears.

At 20,000 feet he picked up the trail of enemy bombers. He was back to his old self. He laughed now, as he remembered the corporal. And suddenly a great truth about this island of Britain struck him, like a revelation: a nation of such imperturbability must win, even if the Germans burned down all its 'Londons.'

Chapter 8

Pain

SECOND LIEUTENANT Jan Daszewski, aka Long Joe to his friends, was in truth a puzzle. He concealed a number of secrets, and people easily misjudged him. Once a British sailor made that mistake. The sailor saw a thin airman with a shy, gentle smile. He decided to borrow Long Joe's girl during a dance. But Joe was not about to let his girl be taken from him; he punched the sailor in the jaw. The hard knock-out punch flattened the interfering sailor, who learned that Daszewski's smile did not preclude a proud soul and iron muscles.

The smile and the very light, very cheerful eyes also hid another secret: no-one would have imagined that Daszewski had been through the fires of hell…

He too had helped himself to a bomber during that turkey shoot of Dorniers on the 7th of September. In the ensuing confusion he had chased the Germans as far as Dover, but there the tables were turned. Jumped by Messerschmitts, he took a round right in his cockpit.

Daszewski was really hit. A piece of shrapnel tore great chunks from his thigh, hip and shoulder—the pain was so acute that it paralysed the right side of his body. At the same time, hot glycol spurted from his radiator, scalding his face. Acrid smoke filled the cockpit.

Despite the shock, Daszewski was still thinking clearly: he must get out of the firing line! Get out, but how? His plane was as badly damaged as Daszewski himself. The control cables had been cut, the joystick swung limply.

His Hurricane fell into a spin. With every turn, a mix of blood, oil and glycol splashed inside the cockpit and, even worse, tore the wounded man's brain in a thousand directions. Daszewski needed to act, and quickly. He had only a few seconds. The plane was spiralling down, down, down. The ground was rushing up to meet it.

There was only one way out: jump. Daszewski opened the canopy, but he could not climb out. He was too weak. The pressure of the slipstream pushed him back, pressing the hatch closed. He struggled like a madman. Finally, with a desperate effort from his good left arm, he managed to scramble to the lip. But here another obstacle barred his path: his lines—the radio and oxygen lines attached to his flying suit. They tethered the fighter pilot to the aircraft. Daszewski strained against them like a chained animal. Finally, summoning his last reserves of energy, he succeeded. He broke the lines. He fell into space.

Two emotions now overtook him: astonishment and fear. Astonishment that he had not hit the tail of his plane, which was easy to do in a spin. Fear that there were Messerschmitts above him. Germans had a habit of firing at enemy parachutes. A great many black crosses were circling nearby. Daszewski was on his guard. He did not open his parachute.

He was dropping in an awkward position: face up and with his back to the ground. He could not see the ground at all, and he was still corkscrewing, his whole body spinning.

From the left: Henneberg and Daszewski

Daszewski, in England, still wears his dark blue French uniform.

A Dornier 215 light bomber, nicknamed 'the flying pencil' because of its thin-shaped fuselage.

Suddenly the spin began to tilt; Daszewski could see an occasional patch of ground at the edge of the whirling sky. But this was only the horizon. Daszewski still could not tell how close he was to the ground. Panic seized him: what if the ground was really close? When had he jumped? How long had he been falling? Minutes, or merely fractions of a second? He tried in vain to twist his neck to see the ground. Falling, falling, heavy as a lump of concrete. He began to count: one, two, three... but soon gave up. His thoughts scattered like smoke, and anyway, why count? His panic mounted. The Messerschmitts no longer existed, the threat of their rounds forgotten. All that existed was this abyss, filled with approaching doom. Enough! Enough of this falling! Open the parachute!

However, the parachute is opened by pulling the ripcord handle with the right hand. But Daszewski could not move his paralysed right arm. He could not open his parachute. He tried with his left arm. In vain. He could not reach it. Death was close, too damn close. But Daszewski did not want to give up. He wanted to live! He began to jerk his left arm as if in a spasm. He must live! He must open the parachute!

The rapid fall from 20,000 feet and the sudden change of pressure were almost tearing out his lungs. Daszewski felt that his head would burst. His left arm continued to jerk spasmodically. Suddenly, in some kind of contortion, he touched metal. The handle! He pulled it. He heard a long swish behind his back. The parachute was opening. Daszewski knew he was saved.

When the parachute opened completely, it jerked Daszewski upright. The jerk caused new pain, so piercing the airman thought he would lose his mind. The parachute harness pressed directly over his wounded hip. The agony got worse by the minute, but there was nothing he could do about it. Despite intense pain, Daszewski did not lose consciousness, indeed quite the opposite, the wind revived him. That was worse.

Finally, he could endure it no longer. He tried to release the straps, though it would have been suicide. Fortunately, he did not have strength enough to succeed. So he continued to fall and suffer.

The parachute had opened at an altitude of around 6,000 feet. An age passed—or so it seemed to Daszewski—and the ground was not getting any closer. The wind began to blow him out to sea. The Pole was now over water, but this new danger meant little to him. Later, much later, a contrary wind blew him back to the coast. He finally landed near a farm. The parachute dragged him along over the hard bumps of ploughed land, but by now Daszewski was indifferent to all pain.

He heard voices. People were chasing after him. They caught his legs and held him. Sheer torture: people pulled his injured leg in one direction, the parachute pulled in another. Seeing the unfamiliar uniform—he was wearing a uniform from his time in France, and his Polish insignia—they called out 'German,' and treated him roughly.

'No German! Polish!' Daszewski protested in a weak voice, and tried to smile.

When his nationality was finally clarified and the unruly parachute dragged to the ground, a new problem arose, namely, how to unhook the airman from it. Nobody knew how to release the harness, and he could not show them. They fiddled, tried, tugged. Daszewski, quite helpless, suffered while they struggled, until at last someone cut the straps with a knife— a simple and ancient way of dealing with the Gordian knot.

Before the ambulance arrived, they bandaged his leg. They were a keen and friendly group, some applied the bandage, while others held him still. A member of the Home Guard, built like an ox, held his right shoulder in an iron grasp exactly on his wound. Daszewski cursed him, implored him, prayed, but in his agony, he had forgotten his English and was whispering in Polish:

'Let go, friend!... Let go my shoulder, you bugger!... My shoulder... God, my shoulder!...'

To no avail. Not until the hefty Home Guard saw blood on his own hands did he look under the torn sleeve. He saw the problem, and let go. He said good-heartedly:

'Oh, I am so sorry!...'

When Daszewski was loaded into the ambulance, he fell into a deep sleep... or more likely, he fainted.

He left hospital three and a half months later. He had lost weight, but the wounds had healed. His muscles were just as hard and his spirit was intact. Daszewski was in the air again hunting for bombers and Messerschmitts.

But the strangest and most striking things about him are his eyes and his smile. Daszewski always has a light in his eyes and a childlike happiness in his smile. His painful experiences and weeks of fever did not break him, left no ugly traces on him. Daszewski simply retained his inward calm.

His invincible vitality is deeply moving, and sometimes, looking at that unbowed lad from the Vistula, one gets the impression that Daszewski is more than a brilliant warrior of the air. He is a symbol of something indestructible. His pain and scars, and his sunlit eyes and smile, are indeed symbols of his victorious, if wounded, nation.

CHAPTER 9

A Smile Through the Blood

SECOND LIEUTENANT Jan Zumbach was flying rear guard.
He was the section's top cover, circling to protect it from above
and behind against a sneak attack. He had his work cut out.
There was a devil of a pack of Messerschmitts up there!
Besides the German fighters already engaged by the
Hurricanes, he could see silhouettes of individual enemy
planes all over the sky, here, there, above him, and even higher,
but some no more than half a mile away.

England was invisible, hidden under dense, uninterrupted
cloud. The fighters flew above a fluffy carpet which glowed in
the September sun. The carpet's magical light and the complete
isolation from earth gave Zumbach the oddest feeling that there
was no ground at all, that everything was happening in a fairy
dreamland. That savage dogfight over here, that fierce battle up
there—nothing but phantoms.

'Phantoms!' Zumbach called out loudly in his cockpit,
then laughed at himself. Zumbach was a sober fighter pilot, not
a dreamer.

He was suddenly alarmed by the disappearance of the
section leader's aircraft. It had been there a moment ago, but

Zumbach had lost sight of him briefly while making a precautionary sweep. Here and there little patches of cloud floated, like scattered bushes in a desert. His leader must have disappeared behind just such a screen. But now, ah yes, he had reappeared, a little higher than before—some 500 yards ahead of Zumbach. Yes, that was definitely his leader, Zumbach decided with relief.

He spurted ahead to catch up swiftly with the leader. Drawing within a few dozen yards, Zumbach throttled back to slot in automatically on his leader's wing when something odd caught his eye: the aircraft ahead of him had two struts, wooden braces, by the horizontal tailplanes. But Hurricanes had none. Zumbach focused intently—after all he had good Polish eyes!—and clearly saw two struts. What the devil?

The Pole was flying directly in line with this strange aircraft. In order to get a better look, he swerved to one side. He was dumbfounded: this aircraft had yellow horizontal stripes and a black cross. A black cross! A Messerschmitt 109!!

The hair bristled on Zumbach's neck and he hunched down. From a little higher up and to one side, without making any adjustments, he spewed out a long burst towards the enemy. At that close range, the rounds tore into the fuselage like blows of a sharp hatchet. Fragments flew off the Messerschmitt, and part of one wing simply fell off. Pouring smoke, the aircraft plummeted down, a flaming torch vanishing into the clouds.

Zumbach watched it go down with blazing eyes.

'Phantoms!' he whispered, just a little surprised, and again he laughed, this time in victory...

He was about to search for his leader again, when out of the sky swooped another Messerschmitt, coming to the rescue of his downed comrade. Zumbach was sweeping around in a circle, which saved him: all the enemy's rounds went wide. He saw them stream past.

Zumbach jumped as if scalded. He climbed to get into a dogfight. But the German was no fool; he refused to take the bait. Exploiting his greater speed, he dived, then climbed sharply to regain his advantage of height. He then dived again, this time firing as he came. Again and again, like an enraged bird, the German pecked at Zumbach. The Pole kept narrowing his turning circle. That was his only defence: it is difficult to hit a plane while it is turning, and the German rounds went wide.

A terrible determination gripped the combatants. One of them would have to die! The German had the upper hand. He was the one firing. Zumbach couldn't fire, he was on the defensive. But as he circled, he slowly gained altitude. With superhuman energy he was drawing closer to his enemy. He knew he was doomed if he could not draw level and fight on equal terms.

Then, hell! Another Messerschmitt joined the first one. The Germans changed tactics. They did not attack. They were now also circling, like Zumbach, but only higher. They appeared to be just watching him. That indeed was what they were doing—watching him.

No end in sight! Two more Messerschmitts appeared! They disappeared again, but they had to be nearby and were up to something. There were now four Messerschmitts. Too many! Zumbach was no longer thinking of joining battle. He had just one thought: to escape, to save himself! To flee into clouds. He looked down and froze; there, beneath him, a Messerschmitt was circling just above the clouds! A fifth one! Escape was cut off.

Jan Zumbach

MESSERSCHMITT 109
[Note the diagonal struts on the tail]

HURRICANE

MESSERSCHMITT 109

HURRICANE

HURRICANE

MESSERSCHMITT 109

SPITFIRE

HURRICANE

SPITFIRE

SPITFIRE

SPITFIRE

SPITFIRE

'...something odd caught his eye: the aircraft ahead of him had two struts, wooden braces, by the horizontal tailplanes. But Hurricanes had none.'

From the left: 303 Squadron mechanic Mozół and Zumbach.

From the left: Zumbach and Daszewski.

From the left: Zumbach, one of the squadron mascots, and Ferić.

From the left: Kustrzyński, Popek (holding a mascot dog), Szlagowski, another of the squadron's pet dogs, Ferić, Daszewski and Zumbach.

Zumbach was a fearless pilot and bold in war, yet at that moment, trapped in this cage of Messerschmitts, he could not stifle a feeling of fear: a cold shiver ran down his spine. But he had nerves of steel, and his brain did not stop working for a moment. He rejected the seemingly attractive idea of making a desperate, wild dive for the clouds. Though the clouds were no more than 1,500 feet below, the experienced airman knew that before he reached them, the Messerschmitts would be on his tail and get him with their first burst. So he chose another route, the only one, although it required inhuman self-control. He did not flee like the devil. He continued to circle, gently dropping towards the clouds. Zumbach was an old hand: he kept firm control over the joystick and his nerves.

It was now clear what the other pair of Messerschmitts were up to. They had slipped out of sight to climb high above him. Now they swooped down on the Hurricane from out of the sun. One dived first, fired and missed. As he was pulling out of his dive to climb back into the sun, the other followed him down. At last Zumbach understood their cunning plan: while three Messerschmitts—two above and one below—were watching his every move to ensure that he did not slip out of the trap, the remaining two would calmly attack and, taking turns, strike the final blow.

Fortunately, the second burst also missed. The third one too. Zumbach had meanwhile lost a considerable amount of altitude; he was now dangerously close to the fifth Messerschmitt.

Suddenly something quite unforeseen happened. A freak act of fickle fate dealt the fighter pilots an extraordinary surprise.

The fourth attack: the German rounds screamed past Zumbach's head, missing him, but passing close to the fifth

Messerschmitt below him. The latter, unclear where the hail of fire had come from, apparently thought some other Hurricane was attacking. The German suddenly broke away and looped into the clouds.

Everything happened in a flash: Zumbach followed his enemy's example. He dived. He was in direct line with the Messerschmitt, less than 300 feet above the German. Instinctively Zumbach got the Messerschmitt in his sights and squeezed the trigger. A hit! The Messerschmitt leapt, then slid helplessly on one wing into the clouds. The Pole followed.

He slipped into the clouds. He had escaped the trap. He was saved. Dazed, shaken, but alive. His aircraft's instruments were also shaken up: neither the compass nor the artificial horizon were working.

When Zumbach landed a quarter of an hour later, on his airfield among his delighted comrades, he immediately asked for a cigarette and a glass of water. His comrades looked anxiously at his parched lips: there were a few drops of dried blood at the edges.

Zumbach smiled at his friends—through the blood.

CHAPTER 10

The Cloud

MAN NO longer looks at clouds as something distant and unobtainable—the source of dreams, or a farmer's anxiety, or a painter's inspiration. Today, clouds have a different significance: deeply enmeshed in human lives, an important element in human fate. For the airman, especially the fighter pilot, clouds are what thick forests used to be for the explorer of distant lands: at times the threat of ambush, at times the blessing of escape. The old backdrop for the romantic stories of James Fenimore Cooper was green and grew on the surface of the earth; in today's romance, it is white and billows in the sky.

Second Lieutenant Jan Zumbach had saved himself by diving into the clouds. Oddly enough, seven or eight miles away and at the same time, another fighter pilot from 303 Squadron, Sergeant Kazimierz Wünsche, had a similar experience. He too had been jumped by several Messerschmitts. He too had dodged their rounds by violent turning. But before the enemy had time to organise an effective hunt, Wünsche broke away and fled into a cloud.

Unfortunately, it was only a single cloud, a huge one, but distant from the others, like an island. It was a spherical cumulus a mile in diameter, flattened at top and bottom.

Wünsche was well hidden within this cloud. Quite safe from his tormentors. He felt relieved. The light grey cotton wool around him was so thick that he could not even see the tips of his own wings. He was now flying blind, relying only on his instruments. He maintained the same altitude and within the cloud made circles about a half mile in diameter.

When, after a few turns, he had calmed down from the recent battle, he began to reason coldly. Escape sideways or up was impossible, since he knew that the Messerschmitts were there. The only way out was down. Wünsche did not hesitate. His Hurricane was running low on fuel, with perhaps another half hour left, so he had to act.

He pushed his stick forward. The pressure forcing his shoulders back immediately told him he was diving. He reached the bottom of the cloud, which was denser and somewhat darker. In the next instant, Wünsche was stunned by the flash of brilliant daylight. He had shot out of the cloud.

Messerschmitts patrolled below. There were five or six, and they were firing at someone in the cloud. Apparently another plane had also been hiding in there. Wünsche had barely covered a hundred yards, when he saw a swirl of tracers around his Hurricane. The Germans were already firing at him! This was not the way out. Wünsche pulled out of his dive and zoomed up. In the rocketing climb, blood drained from his head and he blacked out, but he held onto the stick. Finally, he was back in the cloud, safe again.

The friendly cloud. But this friendliness had a bitter taste for the pilot. For a fighter pilot is like a bird: he must see into the distance, he must see where he is flying. Space is his element. But in a cloud, his eyes are blind. This was unbearable for Wünsche, all the more so because somewhere dangerously

Polish airmen being evacuated from France to England. Kazimierz Wünsche, future 303 Squadron pilot, plays an accordion on board ship.

From the left: Szaposznikow, Karubin and Wünsche.

Wünsche with 303 Squadron mascot 'Misia.'

Mechanic Kwiatkowski checking over Hurricane P3700 RF-E. This is the aircraft from which Wünsche had to bale out, wounded and burnt, on the 9th of September.

nearby he knew another plane was flying blind, just as he was. They were two friends locked in some nightmarish duel, courting death in the mists.

Wünsche was very young, younger than all his comrades. All his life he had dreamt of great flying, of victory in combat, and if he even sometimes thought about death, it would have been a glorious one. Not like this: a stupid, accidental, ignominious death at the hands of a comrade. He felt like a miserable mouse escaping from the claws of a cat, straight into the jaws of a trap.

He took another run at escaping. Not down this time, but sideways. Foiled again! Flying out of the cloud he nearly crashed into two Messerschmitts. A sudden back flip and he was off! Back into the cloud. The Germans never even had time to open fire.

So again the cloud had come to his rescue. Within its gloomy walls, Wünsche flew round in circles. Always in circles. Time flew too: seconds, minutes. He was getting low on fuel... and low on hope. Although the friendly cloud hid him, he began to hate it: a cloud is a treacherous sort of friend, for it is also an enemy. The young airman's soul had no room for this kind of duality. Wünsche began to be afraid, something was coming apart within him. His nerves were going. Now he saw the other plane racing towards him, just like sailors of yore saw the Flying Dutchman...then it vanished. Again and again, the phantom plane appeared in the mists before him, then vanished. Was this an illusion or real? Wünsche did not know, but he was terrified. The hair stood up on the nape of his neck.

Now the cloud was friend no longer; it was frightening. It filled him with dread. It confused his thoughts. Wünsche had one thing on his mind: he must escape from this stifling blindness while he still had time. To break out into the open, to see the sunlit sky and the wide world, the blissful world of the pilot—otherwise he would let go the joystick, give up, go mad: the madness of an explorer lost in a trackless jungle.

Wünsche fought the phantom. He had to save himself. He stopped circling and flew straight. He reached the edge of the cloud, he was out in the sunlight. There was no-one in front of him. He did not look sideways. He was blinded. He flew straight on. A gleam of hope, perhaps he would get away with it...

Suddenly a crash, followed by an enormous gush of heat from the engine. Although he could not see the flames, he knew the engine was on fire. They had got him. The Germans had got him after all!

Hot oil spurted into his face. Wünsche felt weak from the heat, close to fainting. With an effort, he pulled off his restraining straps. He still had enough presence of mind to climb to a greater altitude, and throttle back. He opened the canopy. The rush of air revived him, like a splash of cold water. One more effort...the slipstream did the rest: it tore him from the cockpit.

Immediately on jumping, Wünsche made a serious mistake. He opened his parachute when he should have waited. The enemy was still near. But he caught himself too late; already the canopy was billowing out above him.

This enemy recognised only the law of the jungle in its most brutal form: kill mercilessly, destroy even an unarmed opponent...especially an unarmed opponent. Wünsche, hanging helplessly in his harness, looked up and saw two Messerschmitts approaching. He accepted this as an inevitable result of his mistake. He felt strangely indifferent and fell into a kind of gentle torpor. Apparently the lack of oxygen at this altitude and the shock from the fiery oil in the cockpit were the cause.

After two minutes he came to. He was still falling. He was still alive. And Wünsche was going to live, for three Spitfires had appeared and chased off the Messerschmitts. They were now covering the parachute's descent. The fighter pilot was dropping safely towards the ground and a new life.

It had been a friendly cloud after all. Perhaps he should have trusted it more, hung on longer. But fear had crept into his soul, and destroyed the trust between man and the cloud.

For up there, in the wide open spaces, it was just the same as on the ground: friendship—even friendship between man and nature—was based on the timeless rules of trust.

CHAPTER 11

11th September:
The Greatest Victory

'THE NEXT seven days may decide the issue of the whole war. There never has been a more critical week in world history. The perils of any Nazi attempt to invade Britain at once are manifold. But it is now or never for them. If they flinch, we win.' So wrote J. L. Garvin in the London *Observer* for the week that opened on the 7th of September 1940 with the Luftwaffe's first ferocious raid on London.

The second raid took place the same night, the 7th/8th of September, and new fires broke out near the still burning glow of the earlier ones. Thereafter, night after night hordes of roaring bombers, bold in the darkness, swarmed over the capital. Their objective was clear: to rupture the giant city's vital arteries, to break the spirit of the nine million human beings it harboured and turn them into a hungry, rebellious rabble, thus forcing the British government to capitulate.

Although Hitler's staff nurtured a dream of destroying London, their calculations were off: they had simply not taken into account the sheer size of this human anthill, and—not for the first time—they had failed to grasp the psychology of Britons. The death of a few hundred civilians and, in time,

Heinkel 111 bombers

RAF Northolt, the 11th of September 1940. Seated foreground: Urbanowicz. From the left, visible are: Łokuciewski, Dr. Wodecki (in dark blue French uniform), František, Kent, Paszkiewicz and Walters.

Hurricanes of 303 Squadron ready to join the aerial battle.

CHAPTER 11

several thousand, and the destruction of a couple of hundred streets, was only a drop in the ocean of the remaining streets and millions of human beings. Huge, sluggish, robust London, its anger, not to mention its sense of humour, mounting, every morning would stubbornly 'shake the dust off its shoulders' and continue with business as usual.

During this period of heavy night raids the Luftwaffe also continued its daylight raids, knowing that only a daylight victory could really decide the Battle of Britain. After the painful blows sustained on Saturday the 7th of September, the Germans fell silent during the day on the Sunday, as if licking their wounds, but on Monday they renewed the attack. Once again they lost a great number of aircraft, this time fifty-two, and gained no benefit. The following day there was again a tense silence, after which came fiery Wednesday, the 11th of September.

British Intelligence had for some days been observing feverish and secretive preparations on the other side of the Channel. The Germans were gathering barges and concentrating military forces. Something big was in the wind. Everything pointed to the great invasion of England. The decisive hour was approaching.

On the 11th of September the Luftwaffe carried out a mighty raid, one of the most violent to date.

Around 16:00 hrs., a few small Luftwaffe formations crossed the coast from different directions with the clear aim— as it shortly transpired—of distracting the British defence. For, a few minutes later, the main force arrived, heading straight for London. It was an air armada, consisting of about sixty bombers, Heinkel 111s and Dornier 215s, which were covered both above and behind by about forty Messerschmitt 110s, above which, much higher and more to the rear, were fifty

103

Messerschmitt 109s. With such a strong fighter screen, the German bombers expected to be able to break through to London.

Not all of them got through. Despite the diversion and the Germans' strength, the bombers were mauled en route. That day 303 Squadron had its greatest victory, if not indeed an RAF record. In less than a quarter of an hour, its twelve aircraft shot down seventeen Germans.

303 Squadron was flying on a south-easterly heading, vectored by ground control, when it spotted the bombers already about twelve miles inland. The squadron was flying above the bombers, but below the Messerschmitts.

The situation was very tricky, and indeed there was only one sensible course of action: try to engage the German fighter screen. Especially now that another British fighter squadron at that moment had appeared a little below them, heading to cut off the bombers. However, Flight Lieutenant Forbes, commanding the first section and that day leading the entire squadron, decided to attack the bombers too, despite the enormous risk of flying under a swarm of ninety Messerschmitts.

When the first section, followed by the others, turned towards the bombers at full speed, the obvious happened: the Messerschmitts dived to attack. Before they could get at Forbes and his two wingmen, the second section led by Lieutenant Paszkiewicz hurled itself at the Germans. Like a raised arm, the second section covered their leading comrades. Paszkiewicz, one of the best fighter pilots, and also a fine comrade and a man of character, had instantly realised what was happening. In a ferocious mêlée, the three Poles tackled a dozen or so Messerschmitts. The whirling confusion helped not only the first section, but also Lieutenant Arsen Cebrzyński's third section. They bypassed the dogfight and headed unscathed straight for the bombers, following Forbes. Meanwhile, more Messerschmitts were diving into the fight, but were taken on by Lieutenant Henneberg's fourth section.

This was one of the most memorable episodes of the war: six fighter pilots desperately struggling for their lives, their tenacity appearing to triple their strength, held off a vastly stronger enemy force. By all normal expectations, they should have been instantly crushed, torn to shreds. But unexpectedly, it was they who mauled the enemy. Those six fighter pilots parried the Messerschmitts so effectively that they formed an impenetrable barrier, under whose protection the other six Hurricanes could pounce on the bombers from the rear. At the same time, a fresh British squadron of twelve aircraft, which had just arrived, tore into the leading bombers from the front.

The bomber force, caught between two fires, could not withstand the blow. Not because it suffered heavy losses. Its losses were relatively slight: to be sure Forbes at once shot down a Dornier, Sergeant Michał Brzezowski took down a Heinkel, Sergeant Josef František another Heinkel, while up ahead the British also destroyed two or three bombers. But it was not these hits which decided the battle. The Germans were losing their nerve.

Confident in the overwhelming advantage of their fighter screen, the Germans had never expected such an audacious defence. They were taken quite by surprise. Shaken, they lost their heads. The bombers began hastily to unload their bombs, just as frightened vultures empty the contents of their stomachs. Breaking ranks, they scrambled away in wild panic—some towards France, others blindly towards Ireland. And although the top-cover Messerschmitts immediately dived to chase off the devilish Hurricanes—and did chase them off—no power could stop the panic-stricken bombers.

The panic was general and uncontrollable. The Luftwaffe's great raid broke into paralyzed parts, like the body of a leper.

This was achieved not only by the audacity of eighteen Hurricanes going straight for the bombers, but above all by Paszkiewicz's and Henneberg's six fighter aircraft, which for several dozen seconds—decisive seconds in the battle—delayed and disrupted the whole German fighter screen. Paszkiewicz's determined decision to hit the Messerschmitts at just the right moment, and the daring execution of his decision, were like grains of sand thrown into the cogs of a giant machine: they gummed up the works.

After the raid had been broken up, the second and final phase of the battle followed: chasing and destroying the fleeing Germans. Other British squadrons also took part in the chase, joining the six Poles who had been tangling with the German fighter screen and who, by some miracle, had managed to escape the claws of the Messerschmitts. An odd pursuit—given the Luftwaffe's initial superiority in numbers, it was not always clear who was chasing whom.

It was an heroic battle, fought over several counties from London to the Channel coast. The Polish fighter pilots of 303 Squadron once again gave proof of their valiant courage, fearless tenacity and exceptional flying skill. They wreaked havoc, aroused astonishment and conquered.

The Poles strewed the fields with fragments of every type of German aircraft then flying over England: Heinkels, Dorniers, Messerschmitt 109s and 110s. Two pilots from 303 Squadron each shot down one aircraft, six had two each, and a ninth had three in short order. Sergeant Szaposznikow had a real double strike: he chased down two Messerschmitt 110s flying close together, shot both rear gunners and then with the same burst of fire swept both aircraft almost simultaneously

The destruction of a Hurricane in
aerial combat over the English coast.

A hail of fire from a Messerschmitt 109
has torn off the port wing of the fighter
and the pilot has baled out—his parachute
is just beginning to open (top centre of
picture).

This dramatic photograph was taken
from a Messerschmitt equipped with
an automatic film camera.

303 Squadron operations officer Giejsztowt with the letter of the 20th of September 1940 from Chief Officer F. C. Paige of Westerham Fire Brigade, referring to the brave death of Sergeant Wójtowicz.

SEVENOAKS RURAL DISTRICT COUNCIL

WESTERHAM FIRE BRIGADE

To Flying Officer E. H. L. Hadwen
No. 303 Polish Squadron
RAF Northolt   Sept. 20th, 1940

Dear Sir,

May I thank you for telling No. 303 Polish Squadron what little we in Westerham did for their comrade Sgt. Pilot Wojtowicz, and if at any time another of them are unfortunate to have a mishap in or near our town we will do all in our power to help him.

As to your question about Sgt. Pilot Wojtowicz putting up a good fight, there is no doubt about it for he fought magnificently, and there is also no doubt about him bringing down the two Me 109s. As you can see by the enclosed statements which I myself and a Special Constable have signed as we two stood and watched the fight with other men of the A.R.P.

Yours faithfully,
F. C. Paige

Contents of the letter from Chief Officer Paige.

From the left: Kowalski, František, Bełc, Paszkiewicz and squadron mechanic Mikołajczak.

The grave of Arsen Cebrzyński.

out of the sky. Other British squadrons, which had now joined the fray, also had a decent harvest.

Two Poles were killed in this battle. They died like heroes. The first was Cebrzyński who, leading his section against the bombers, got caught in the crossfire from German gunners; he was hit in the head and died instantly. The second one, Sergeant Stefan Wójtowicz, attacked by nine Messerschmitts, fought like a wildcat. The Germans, despite superiority in numbers, could not catch him. The whole population of Biggin Hill, watching the battle, had its heart in its mouth. Wójtowicz shot down two enemy aircraft before the others riddled his Hurricane with rounds. This Polish sergeant's dogfight became a legend in the little English town.

As I have already mentioned, the fighter pilots of 303 Squadron destroyed seventeen German aircraft, more than 25 percent of the sixty-one shot down that day by the RAF. The Germans were not easy prey. The fighting was exceptionally savage, as shown by the great percentage of British losses that day, compared to other days: twenty-four aircraft shot down and seventeen pilots killed.

Thus the German hopes ended in a resounding defeat that day, a day in the most 'critical week in world history.' And a day of new glory for 303 Squadron. A handful of fighter pilots, some of Churchill's famous 'few,' had gallantly turned the tide. The German invasion barges waited in vain for their orders.

And that night, when the German bombers again approached London under cover of darkness, they were in for a new surprise. They ran into a murderously fierce barrier of anti-aircraft fire. Suddenly out of the night hundreds of guns belched fire. Not a bomb fell on London. For the first time in several nights, the capital slept peacefully.

CHAPTER 12

The Enemy's Dance of Death

EXPERIENCED HUNTERS, well versed in the forest and the habits of animals, know on which trails to lay an ambush. Hunters in Hurricanes and Spitfires also know the best place to catch their prey: over the Channel, where tired Germans return from England to France after raids which may or may not have been successful. The fighter pilots of 303 Squadron, after carrying out their duty as a team, liked to rush to the Channel coast and lie in wait. This was a pleasant and worthwhile sport, which the squadron called 'the František method.'

That is what Second Lieutenant 'Tolo' Łokuciewski did on that glorious day, the 11th of September, when 303 Squadron shot down seventeen enemy aircraft. Tolo was a member of those brave six who had engaged and so effectively blocked the whole swarm of Messerschmitts. But in a fight with some 'little Adolf,' Tolo had a difficult time of it. He lost contact with the squadron, and when he eventually shot down the German, he was already near the Channel. There was no point in rejoining his comrades; they had scattered all over the sky. Therefore, he decided to lie in wait off the coast, in case something turned up.

It was worth it. After a few minutes he spotted the silhouette of a Dornier 215 in the distance returning from somewhere inland. The bomber was much lower than Tolo's Hurricane, and heading straight for him. Tolo smiled, and his face—such a youthful face—lit up with pleasure. A solitary bomber was an almost certain kill for the Hurricane.

His first attack, from a steep head-on dive, was unsuccessful. Clearly Tolo's aim was off in this difficult firing position. After passing the Dornier, Tolo climbed, flipped backwards and now attacked from a better position, from the rear and the side. He raked the bomber's fuselage, silencing the rear gunner. The German twisted desperately to save himself. To no avail. Tolo had already put a few well-aimed bursts into the Dornier's starboard engine. The engine began to smoke, faintly at first, but soon more heavily. Then followed a scene which filled Tolo with awed amazement. And with silent delight. The enemy began his dance of death. A swan song waltzed in loops and arcs across the sky, the crazy minuet of some fatally wounded madman.

First the Dornier climbed. Rising in a vast sweep, gracious, broad and gradually slowing, like a pathetic attempt to escape from earthly afflictions. It seemed to soar endlessly. But the higher it flew, the more it laboured, until somewhere above, at an invisible peak, its impetus slackened. The bomber paused in a theatrical gesture of doubt. A moment passed. Then it began to fall back on its port wing, faltering, clearly swooning. It shifted gently onto its head and fell helplessly into a vertical dive. An expression of demonic lunacy, racing straight to earth, writing its own death sentence in the air.

Witold 'Tolo' Łokuciewski

From the left: Łokuciewski, Ferić, Kent, Grzeszczak, Zumbach, Radomski and Henneberg.

General Sikorski at RAF Northolt, the 18th of September 1940, decorating 303 Squadron pilots with the Silver Cross of the Virtuti Militari. Visible in the line-up of pilots are Henneberg, Paszkiewicz, Ferić and Łokuciewski (*being decorated*), next to him (*on the right*) is Zumbach, František and Szaposznikow.

The bomber fell several thousand feet in a few seconds. But not all the way.

Mid-way through its fall to earth, the Dornier pulled out of the dive and, turning away, cheated death by the narrowest margin. Again it rose on some extraordinary parabola, with seeming new life and energy; having gathered exceptional momentum, it climbed again to an incredible altitude. It was flying to the top of some soaring mountain, some glorious summit—both the summit and the aircraft were full of heart-rending pathos.

Tolo followed the bomber's evolutions with bated breath. Fighter pilots have a highly developed sense of the poetry of motion. After all, aerobatics are a staple of their armoury, and aerobatics are really a dance. They are a constant improvisation of gracefulness, something fighter pilots thoroughly appreciate. So Tolo watched the spectacle, at first with astonishment and then with growing elation. He had long ceased firing. There was no need to fire. Tolo flew aside and watched. He drank in the beauty of the nameless movement and tasted its wild magic.

This lasted but a moment. Once again Tolo was all business, and his delight turned into a soldier's pleasure. Here was a haughty enemy who had come to kill and destroy, who everywhere had killed and destroyed, in Poland and elsewhere. Now for him, a Polish fighter pilot, this arrogant enemy was dancing the barren dance of an impotent witch. The German, powerless in his rage and fear, struggled mightily, but he was unable to break the invisible net in which he was caught. In his arrogance he had thought he could tear the world apart, trampling everything in his path. Now it was he who danced like a trapped beast, a wild creature wounded by a fatal arrow, held on a magic leash. Unable to escape, he danced like a madman—and in his crazed dance, he unconsciously paid homage to his conqueror.

Tolo guessed what had happened. Not only had he damaged one engine, but he had probably also seriously wounded the German pilot, who still gripped the stick and through it transmitted to the whole aircraft the convulsions of his own agonies. Tolo kept his eyes on the Dornier. Although the spectacle fully engaged his imagination, his thumb continued to hover over the trigger of his machine guns, ready to send a new burst into the enemy.

But there was no need. It was his enemy's final dance, his last climb. After again reaching a dead point, the bomber slid back onto its tail and fell into a reverse corkscrew. Yet another dance from the zenith into the abyss, a long rosary of giddy pirouettes. And then the end. The Dornier slammed into the sea a few hundred yards from shore, turned onto its nose, and sank with its entire crew. The sea closed over it like a final stage curtain.

The Muslim faithful make the pilgrimage to Mecca from far-distant lands, and on the way they dance. The road to Poland was longer and more laborious than the one to Mecca. It was twisting, convoluted, with many bypaths and sown with thorns, yet glorious and often trodden in a dance. The dance of death.

Somewhere along the thousands of turns in this road, like a white milepost, stood the rocky cliffs of the English Channel, silent witness to aerial dances and the irresistible attraction of 'the František method' for the fighter pilots of 303 Squadron.

CHAPTER 13

A Brave Czech

THIS COCKY Czech was a black sheep among his own people; he was not level-headed, he was not polished. In fact, he was out of place in modern times: he had the exhilaration of a romantic, the ardour of the Middle Ages, and he was like a volcano spewing lava onto all the wrong places. He hoed his own row, took his own path. Such people are rare these days. They either die as criminals, or become heroes. Josef František became a hero.

When the Germans entered Prague in March 1939, he was a Czech sergeant pilot and one of a brave handful who actively protested against that act of rape: he stole an aircraft and flew to Poland. He did this in defiance of his own authorities, in defiance of the community and 'common sense': after all, he could have continued to live quietly and peacefully in the Protectorate, like so many others. But František did not want to live peacefully. He wanted to fight. He had to fight. His exuberant personality and proud nature could not reconcile themselves to rapacious totalitarianism and subjugation to the

Germans. So František, true to himself, flew off to the site of future battles and linked his fate to that of the Poles.

He lived through their whole nightmare. Tragic September 1939 and the road to Zaleszczyki,[1] Romania and the Balkan odyssey. The Mediterranean and France. Still among them, still one of them. Not just a fellow countryman and not just a fellow Slav; but, just like them, determined and desperate. This was the strongest of bonds: together with the Poles he fiercely sought a new weapon against their common enemy and hungered for a new battleground. This is what linked them.

They found both in France. Unfortunately, as we know, the short-lived fire of the French campaign was snuffed out almost before it had ignited. But in that short time another flame flared up—František's fame. An eternal flame. The Czech showed his true colours, those of an outstanding pilot and superb hunter. In aerial combat over Belgium and Champagne he shot down ten German aircraft in three weeks.[2] Then came the fall of France. Again František's weapon was knocked from his hands, again he searched feverishly for another. This led to Bordeaux, the Bay of Biscay and England.

In England, fate harnessed František to 303 Squadron once and for all, come hell or high water. But above all for victory. He played a distinguished role in all of the squadron's major battles. Starting on the 2nd of September, he scored successes almost every day; many times he downed two and

---

[1] This was the border town through which many Polish military units escaped to Romania in September 1939. Translator's note.

[2] In the autumn of 1940, the British press reported that František had shot down as many as eleven aircraft in France, but for the sake of accuracy we should point out that one of the most distinguished fighter pilots of 303 Squadron questioned this number in 1965. Author's note.

Josef František

From the left: František, Kowalski, Wojciechowski (*behind*), Paszkiewicz, Bełc and Żak.

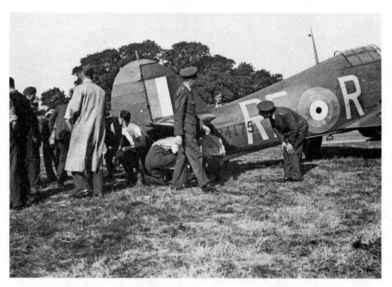

Engineering officers and mechanics inspect damage to the tail of Hurricane R4175 RF-R. This was František's lucky aircraft, in which he scored seven victories.

sometimes three enemy aircraft in a single sortie. František almost never returned without a kill, advancing in a triumphal procession from success to success.

In the early days of the Battle of Britain there was an unpleasant hiccup. Through František's fault, the leader of his section was almost killed. During an attack on several Messerschmitts, the leader was dismayed to see at the last moment that František was no longer beside him, but had inexplicably broken ranks and disappeared. This jeopardised the whole plan of attack, and the rest of the section was forced to make a hasty withdrawal. When František returned to base, it turned out that after breaking away he had shot down two Germans near the Channel.

But when over the next few days he broke ranks again and again, the matter started to become serious. Team discipline is an essential element of air combat. The commander—whether of a flight, a squadron or a wing—must be able to rely unconditionally on his fighter pilots. Otherwise disorder and chaos reign. František was causing disorder.

After another such episode, he was summoned to appear before the Polish Squadron OC Urbanowicz. František stood stiffly to attention before his superior officer. He always stood stiffly; he was a handsome young man, with a fearless eye and an endearing confidence. He explained that if he saw some son of a gun with black crosses off to the side he could not bear it. He just had to get that German. The urge to dash after that enemy was stronger than he could control.

'My friend,' said Urbanowicz calmly, his voice as sharp as steel, 'the squadron is indeed glad to have such a fine fighter pilot in its midst, but there is one thing we cannot forget: we are soldiers and as such have to do our duty. I must firmly insist that you not break ranks before an engagement.'

'Yessir!'

He sounded quite sincere, and indeed František was sincere... at that moment. For two days all went well. Then once again the devil intervened and František returned to his old ways. At 15,000 feet he began to feel anxious, at 18,000 he could stand it no longer. He disappeared, heading for the Channel.

Over the Channel František was in heaven: he would lie in wait for Germans returning from their raids over England. They usually appeared in scattered formations, often maimed, and always on their last drops of fuel. It was easy then to finish them off. The Channel coast became a real threshold of death for many a German marauder.

'The František method,' as this hunt along the coast was called in 303 Squadron, had a great many adherents among the Poles and also among British pilots. But there was a difference between the others and František: the others dashed for the Channel only after carrying out their assigned mission; while František frequently fought alongside them, he would more often head directly for the coast immediately after take-off.

This was his craze, his secret vice, his addiction, his irresistible passion. It was not simply a matter of destroying the greatest number of Germans; it was something deeper, something in František's soul. He was a fine drinking companion, a good friend at all times, with women he was a thoughtful and generous lover—but in the air he found fulfilment alone, by himself. There he did not recognise company, he hated being confined, he broke all bonds. Like the great eagles, up in the sky František flew solitary, predatory, jealous of his space. He was unwilling to share the air or his victories with anyone.

Of course, František's behaviour undermined the squadron's discipline. This was causing a growing problem for his superiors. Could they remove from the squadron such an outstanding ace and one who brought the unit such glory? Things were clearly headed in that direction, had not his superiors found a solution truly worthy of Solomon, a sensible and also a generous one: the Poles appointed the Czech sergeant a guest of the squadron. A guest was granted unusual independence. The positive results of this wise decision became immediately apparent; his fellow fighter pilots breathed a sigh of relief. And František? František reacted in his own way: the next day he downed three Germans.

One day he had to make a forced landing on some airfield in the South of England. The Czech turned to the Englishmen running toward him:

'I am Polish!' he exclaimed.

František was no renegade, and he always felt himself to be Czech. He was simply underscoring the fact that he belonged to a Polish squadron, and proved emphatically that he was with the Poles, body and soul.

And indeed he was one of them with all his heart. Their temperament better suited his impetuous nature. The British, to whom he was some semi-mythical character, were impressed with František and did their best to persuade him to join one of their squadrons. To no avail. František was not interested in privileges or promotion. He wanted to be with the Poles in their by now famous 303 Squadron; remarkably, he was not even attracted to the Czech fighter squadron which was then forming.

František was, of course, a superb pilot and marksman. He also had an exceptionally cool head and lightning reflexes, as demonstrated in an incident watched by a whole British airfield. During one of the many air battles over Kent, František so badly mauled a Messerschmitt 110 that the

German indicated that he would surrender and land on a nearby airfield. So František ceased firing. The Messerschmitt lowered his undercarriage and started to lose altitude. But it was only a trick. The Messerschmitt's wheels were almost touching the ground, when the German suddenly opened his throttle and shot back up like a spring. He did not get far. At almost that same moment, František put such a burst of fire into the Messerschmitt that he fell like a lead weight, crashing onto the airfield—another laurel in the brave sergeant's wreath.

Towards the end of September, something started to go wrong in František's nervous system. His condition took an odd form: he was flying a great deal, more than ever before, because he felt safe only in the air. On the ground he was tense. During German night raids, he would leap up at the sound of the air raid siren, the first to run to the shelter—he, who before had laughed at such safety precautions.

This new craze seized him as strongly as had all the others. There was something very moving about him, something evoking the deepest pity: the young swashbuckler, who with extraordinary daring and nerves of steel would launch himself at his enemy in the air was, when returning a moment later to base, afraid of the ground.

He grew more and more afraid of the earth, as if the ground were a demon taking its revenge on a man who had fallen so wildly in love with the sky. In this soul full of passionate impulses, in this soul of an unusually fine fighter pilot, a tragedy was brewing, and one whose epilogue came soon enough.

On the 8th of October, František, returning from a sortie, carelessly struck a mound of earth with a wing while doing a traditional victory roll. He crashed, and was killed instantly.

This tragic end reportedly came within sight of the home of his lady-love in Ruislip, near the airfield at RAF Northolt.

Thus, as he had feared, the ground took his life—one of the war's greatest aces, Sergeant Josef František, who had shot down twenty-seven enemy aircraft: ten in France and seventeen in England, and been awarded the Distinguished Flying Medal, the Cross of Valour, the Virtuti Militari and the Czechoslovak War Cross.

František was an indomitable Czech, who when his homeland fell, found a new home in Poland; a leading Czech fighter pilot who wanted to fight and did fight only among Polish fighter pilots. Together they showed the world how, at a moment of crisis, in a decisive battle with a tenacious foe, Poles and Czechs could stand together, shoulder to shoulder, positively and victoriously—and they showed this long before theoretical principles of Polish–Czech relations were addressed around the diplomats' negotiating table.

CHAPTER 14

The Colourless Roots of Brilliant Flowers

LOOK DEEP into the heart of a Polish fighter pilot and you will find great affection, not only, and not always, for his fellow pilot with whom he shares the bonds of combat and destiny. You will also find there the deepest affection for, and a genuine attachment to, that colourless group of men known as 'the ground crew.' The fighter pilot has dedicated his most secret emotions to these men, these mechanics, to whom he owes almost more than to his fellow pilots. Indeed, to these mechanics he owes his life, his victories, his fame.

And his boundless faith in his machine. When a fighter pilot sprawls on a sofa waiting to be scrambled, in his flying suit and Mae West,[1] dozing until the telephone calls him to action, he is strangely calm and carefree. Above, the dangerous and vast Unknown awaits him. But the fighter pilot is not afraid. For he is strong. Strong in the knowledge that while he rests, a mysterious rite of loving care and attention is being

---

[1] Mae West was a popular, and particularly well-endowed, Hollywood actress of the era. Airmen nicknamed their inflatable life jackets 'Mae Wests' for obvious reasons. Translator's note.

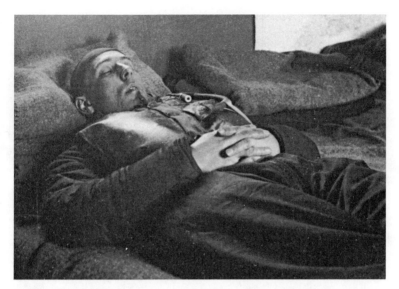

Henneberg rests between sorties, wearing his Mae West over his flying suit.

303 Squadron mechanic Mozół, leaning on the propeller of a Hurricane.

Colourless roots—
303 Squadron mechanics.

performed on his aircraft: the mechanics' ceaseless ministra-
tions. At take-off, the mechanics will bring him a machine
on which he can absolutely rely, without hesitation. This
confidence in his weapon's infallibility becomes a guarantee of
his success.

When a fighter pilot returns from a successful sortie, he
announces the good news to his mechanics with an exuberant
victory roll over their heads. This is both a signal and a tribute
to them. When a moment later the aircraft touches down, they
get a thumbs-up and a big grin. They get his first impressions
of the battle and—strange to tell—it is they who swell with the
greatest pride, pleasure and happiness. Just as if they have
won the victory themselves. And they are correct: it is their
aircraft, lovingly repaired and maintained, which has brought
the victory.

The pilot and his mechanics are filled with a single,
common and profound emotion: they passionately love their
aircraft. But while the mechanics put their hearts and souls
into this love, asking nothing in return, the pilot takes it
all: he dances the aircraft into the air as if it were a girl, he
basks in glory, he earns the laurels. Like a dazzling flower
or a delicious fruit, the pilot arouses universal admiration,
garnering songs, honours and a brilliant place in the sun.
His mechanics are like the humble roots—essential, of course,
for the life of that radiant flower or luscious fruit, but buried
in the shadows, without sunlight, without honours. Just
colourless roots.

Surely there is no other part of the military in which
these colourless roots are as important as in the air force.
When a pilot climbs out of his machine after a sortie, he gives
it not another thought until his next take-off. He throws it into
the arms of his mechanics. Now it is their turn. It is time for

their effort, for their willing and so vital work. It is not just a question of rearming the aircraft as quickly as possible; filling it with fuel, oil, glycol; charging the oxygen cylinders; replacing batteries; testing the instruments. There is more: after all, the complex beast may be sick. A few minutes ago it was violently twisting and turning, diving and climbing through the sky, flexing steel muscles in the most stressful contortions—has it suffered from the strain? Like a human being, it can have secret, treacherous and dangerous ailments, which are worse than open wounds caused by enemy fire.

Thus the mechanic rushes over and begins checking the plane with the most passionate attention to detail. He taps, he feels, he sniffs; he listens and diagnoses—no longer a simple soldier, an aircraftman or a corporal, but a doctor specialising in metal disease, conscious that both the pilot's life, and success in the next battle, depend on the mechanic's skill and efforts. A squadron's victories are born on earth, through the midwifery of its mechanics.

The Polish air mechanic takes his rightful place next to the Polish fighter pilot whose daring has earned the world's admiration. Unsurpassed in his skill, light years better than many foreign mechanics, he puts the lie to the legend that Poles only make good farmers. Even Henry Ford has stressed the Poles' creative talent, praising them as the smartest mechanics in his factories. He is not mistaken.

And now they passed the test of a lifetime. Like other Polish soldiers, they had escaped over the frontier, weathered the French campaign, and arrived in England. There, after only three weeks—amazingly—they had fully mastered the Hurricane's secrets and were servicing the aircraft as if they had known it for years.

It is an irrefutable fact, well-confirmed by the pilots themselves, that the remarkable achievements of 303 Squadron in September 1940 were due in large part to its mechanics. To their resourcefulness, efficiency, skill and devotion. To their days and nights of non-stop work, sometimes without any respite at all. In some cases, badly damaged aircraft that would normally have been returned to the factory, were repaired instead in the squadron's workshops. If this had been any other ground crew, the squadron would have pulled out of the line by mid-September for lack of aircraft. But 303 Squadron never for a moment left the battle. And despite almost daily combat, it always started out with a full complement of twelve aircraft (hence the squadron's records!), with the exception of just four instances: two when it could put up only nine aircraft, and one when it could field only six.

The fourth such instance occurred on the memorable 15th of September. Twelve planes scrambled for the first sortie. The second time it was nine; the third time, towards the end of the day, barely four. During the third sortie no enemy was encountered: the Luftwaffe had already been scattered and driven out of England. That evening, after a victorious day, the squadron's aircraft presented a pitiful spectacle. Ten planes were unfit to fly. They had suffered all sorts of damage—tail fins riddled, glycol radiators smashed, control cables cut, wings and engine cowlings holed, even the propellers shot up. On one plane, a wing was almost sheared off at the fuselage.

The damage was clearly more than the squadron's workshops could handle. And yet the mechanics did not lose heart. Everyone expected the Germans to return the following day in even greater numbers. The mechanics understood just how much now depended on them. They went to work, and they worked all night. No-one gave any orders, for at moments like that orders are unnecessary. It was no longer about them, the mechanics, but about the squadron's very existence. The fervour of inspiration sustained them. Their fingers grew wings. They triumphed. Hard as it is to believe, the impossible became fact: by dawn on the 16th, twelve aircraft were once again ready to fly.

That day of glory for the British and Polish fighter pilots brought a night of glory for the Polish mechanics.

Their commander, Lieutenant Wiórkiewicz, had been one of the leading aircraft engineers in Poland before the war. Honest, all heart, with a kind word for everyone and with an endearing sincerity, he was also a consummate professional with an almost fanatical work ethic. Passion for his work burned like a constant flame within him. His enthusiasm never waned. Such a man had the character to inspire others—and he did inspire them. It is difficult to describe Wiórkiewicz's contribution to 303 Squadron: it was priceless. It is hard to imagine a victorious 303 without him and his mechanics.

Yet the mechanics are merely colourless roots, buried in the shadows. Soldiers, of course, but somehow inferior. Before the war, any arrogant but ignorant infantryman, uhlan or gunner looked down on the lowly mechanic. Now he saw things in a new light. War had taught him to respect the mechanic. Opinions had changed, but the spirit of military regulations had not yet caught up. In this outdated view, mechanics were still second-class soldiers; their work not worthy of honours. No Virtuti Militari or Cross of Valour for them.

The citation for these decorations states clearly that they are awarded for valour 'in the face of the enemy.' Of course, airfields must be located a distance from the front if they are to fulfil successfully their allotted role. So the thousands of mechanics—each squadron had between 150 and 200 ground

Armourer loads ammunition belts into machine gun magazines.

Mechanic working on a Hurricane engine.

Fitter Tadeusz Cedrowski
reaches down to pick
up some engine parts.

303 Squadron 'papa' Żyborski (*on the left*) and an RAF officer.

Engineering Officer Wiórkiewicz (*standing, front, third from right*) with his 303 Squadron mechanics and pilot Andruszków (*standing, front, on the left*).

Dr. Wodecki (*on the right*) with another Polish medical officer.

Giejsztowt (*on the right*) with an RAF officer.

crew members—can never fulfil this basic requirement, and are thus ineligible for gallantry awards. A deplorable misunderstanding prevents ground crew from being honoured, although on them depends success in decisive air combat, and let us be frank here, final victory in this gigantic war.

But medals and crosses are not for mechanics. Unless by some inexcusable blunder on the part of others the enemy breaks through to an airfield. Perhaps then, when a German bomber accidentally finds itself over an airfield and drops its bombs on the ground crew. Then, for keeping one's head in the few seconds of mayhem: a medal. But for the endless devotion and toil, for the lethal reliability of the weapons most critical to the battle, for a real contribution to decisive victory: nothing.

Military decorations, not only Polish but those of all armies, were created at a time when the sword literally decided the issue, and when wars were won exclusively in heroic combat with the enemy hand-to-hand, face-to-face. Although in modern warfare hand-to-hand combat still remains an important factor of victory, it is not the only factor; there are others, equally important and indispensable.

The battle front today extends to areas unknown to commanders of old; it has crept into previously unimaginable fields, it has overturned hoary and long-cherished traditions of war and even ideas of military honour and has, like today's strategy, seen revolutionary changes. In the past, all that mattered was sheer courage finding its expression in face-to-face combat. Today, in a total war in which thousands of tons of steel stand between opponents facing one another, not to mention terrible new arsenals of psychological warfare—today potential courage is just as important, if not more important, for eventual victory. The hidden courage of the supporting arms.

No-one denies that victorious staff officers are entitled to the highest military honours if their work contributes to the enemy's defeat, despite the fact that they work far from the actual fighting. The air mechanics are no different; their work, even if behind the actual front line, contributes directly, very directly, to the enemy's defeat.

And not just the mechanics' work, but the work of the entire ground crew. We have to accept the fact that a fighter squadron, with its phenomenal flexibility, range and firepower, has greater striking power than any infantry brigade of 1914.

If, as General Sikorski has said, the victories of 303 Squadron have brought glory and renown to the reputation of the Polish forces worldwide, it is because every single member of the squadron has done his duty with extraordinary devotion. For it is not just the mechanics who contribute to the pilots' success. It is also the adjutant, Captain Witold Żyborski, who functions as the unit's 'papa'; it is the doctor, Zygmunt Wodecki, who gathers up his injured pilots from all across the South of England; it is Captain Jarosław Giejsztowt, who bears the crucial responsibility of overseeing operations in fighter control.

They all deserve our deepest gratitude. But more, they deserve the highest distinctions: military honour and a basic sense of justice demand it.

CHAPTER 15

A Fearless, Flawless Airman

IT WAS often said that this air war did not produce any outstanding aces, that it was exclusively a team effort. To be sure, dozens of aircraft were fighting together, later hundreds would take to the skies and even later, by the end of the war, there would be thousands. And to be sure, all air battles begin as a team affair. But almost immediately the ranks dissolve, individual fighters attack individual bombers or fighters. Then paradoxically, the most modern weapon, the aeroplane, reverts to mediaeval tactics; battles are decided in a series of individual duels, face-to-face. Here in the air, the strongest personality wins—whether sergeant or colonel, only the strongest will survive. And in the crucible of such intensely personal duels is forged the best of these strong men: the ace.

Some of the pilots of 303 Squadron—Henneberg, Paszkiewicz, Zumbach, Ferić, Łokuciewski, Daszewski, Szaposznikow, Karubin, František—are undoubted aces. Their numerous victories are no accident. And it is no accident that the most outstanding of them is Witold Urbanowicz, victor in seventeen encounters with the enemy.

Anyone who knows him personally is faced with something of a puzzle. It is impossible to fit Urbanowicz into any known pattern; he is beyond human experience. Everything about him is the same as the other fighter pilots: an upright bearing, an energetic face and a clear eye, and yet one feels that there is more. One feels something quite new, some hitherto undiscovered human trait which has no history and no comparison. And then a flash of inspiration: metal. Yes, clearly the personification of metal. The gleam in his light eyes, the clear resonance of his voice, the liveliness of his movements—these are like aluminium, light and strong, which if it were to acquire a human body and soul, must surely have resulted in Urbanowicz. No great surprise then that there is such a highly developed bond between Urbanowicz and his aircraft.

Like most of the pilots in 303 Squadron, he was a professional airman. In the summer of 1940, he was 32 years old and a lieutenant in the Polish Air Force. During the grim days of September 1939, Urbanowicz had an outstanding record of devotion to duty. As an instructor and staff member of the Polish Air Force College at Dęblin, at the outbreak of war he was ordered to take his squad of fifty cadet-officers and escape into Romania, to train them there on French aircraft. Urbanowicz crossed the frontier with his squad on the 17th of September 1939, but after settling his men in a safe place, he immediately returned to Poland to fight. Unfortunately, he was too late. He was captured by Soviet forces, escaped the first night, re-crossed the frontier and, after a three-day absence, caught up with his cadet-officers.

The following weeks were a saga of ruses, evasive action, captures and escapes, endless escapes, and complicated strategy, at the heart of which was always Urbanowicz,

Witold Urbanowicz

Urbanowicz standing on the wing of a Hurricane, his hand in his pocket.

Urbanowicz (*on the left*) describes tactics to Kent.

until eventually he achieved a near-impossibility: he safely loaded all his men onto a ship at Constanţa. They sailed from Romania to Syria, and then to France, where Urbanowicz, the exemplary commander and tireless chaperone, handed over to the Polish authorities almost his entire squad—the most priceless of war matériel. He is one of those commanders who, in difficult days, devotedly and conscientiously took care of his men.

In January 1940, Urbanowicz was posted to England.

He shot down his first German in mid-August, serving at the time with a British RAF squadron. That day he had volunteered to fly as thirteenth man, bringing up the rear and covering his comrades. They were over the sea, near Portsmouth. The enemy was already over the harbour when Urbanowicz spotted four Messerschmitts coming from behind—three to starboard and one to port—overtaking the squadron.

There, in his first encounter with the enemy, the Polish fighter pilot proved his excellent judgment in a tight spot and his lightning reactions. The wrong move could have been fatal for him and the squadron. In an instant, Urbanowicz identified and executed a brilliant strategy: he attacked the three Messerschmitts with such fury that he scared their pilots and scattered the trio. Then he turned sharply to attack the fourth German who, rather than stand and fight, fled. A mad chase ensued. At its climax, his opponent streaked into a swarm of several dozen slowly circling Messerschmitts with Urbanowicz hot on his tail. Quarry and hunter burst out the other side of the swarm so quickly that no-one had time to take on the Pole. The escaping German did everything to shake off his pursuer, to no avail. Eventually the Hurricane's eight guns found their mark, and the German tumbled into the sea.

This first air battle highlighted all the qualities which were to make Urbanowicz so famous in subsequent successes: his excellent judgment, his speed of reaction, his courage and his persistence.

Shortly afterwards, he joined 303 Squadron. On the 7th of September he assumed command, replacing the badly burned Major Krasnodębski. At this time, 303 Squadron was on the verge of its greatest achievements, and Urbanowicz would earn his laurels with it. In the second half of September, with the Luftwaffe clearly losing momentum and signs of fatigue evident on both sides, Urbanowicz really spread his wings, demonstrating his extraordinary resilience, that aluminium stamina of his. And more besides: the rapacity of a bird of prey. In three days, he shot down nine German aircraft. Above all, the last day, the 30th of September, abounded in epic moments.

Urbanowicz was leading the squadron over southern Kent against thirty German bombers. They broke up the German formation, and Urbanowicz himself took on a Dornier 215 which dodged into a cloud, trailing light smoke. Then, a game of hide-and-seek—so skilfully did the Dornier use the cover of small clouds that it began to pull away from the fighter. But over the Channel they struck a wide band of open sky. Swiftly Urbanowicz closed the distance between him and his wounded prey.

But nearby he spotted two Messerschmitts returning to France. Although their presence was coincidental, they prevented Urbanowicz from finishing off the bomber. He had to deal first with the Messerschmitts, who had not yet noticed him. Urbanowicz sneaked up behind the unsuspecting German fighters to within a range of a few dozen yards—intentionally close so that they could not turn and attack him directly. With

146

Urbanowicz (*on the left*) and a squadron mechanic.

Urbanowicz in a contemplative moment.

The 15th of December 1940 at Leconfield, Air Vice-Marshal Sir William Sholto Douglas decorates leading Polish aces of 303 Squadron with the British Distinguished Flying Cross.

Urbanowicz

Henneberg

Zumbach

Ferić

POLAND

King George VI visits 303 Squadron at RAF Northolt on the 26th of September 1940. *From the left:* Air Vice-Marshal Sir Keith Park, Urbanowicz, King George VI (reading the victories of 303 Squadron) and Kellett.

King George VI shakes hands with Forbes. Also visible in the line-up in front are are Urbanowicz (*to the left*) and Paszkiewicz and Żak (*to the right*).

a long burst, Urbanowicz set the first Messerschmitt aflame, and then sent the second careening into the sea before the German knew what had happened. The way to the bomber was now clear.

Meanwhile, the Dornier was approaching the French coast, losing altitude. Urbanowicz pursued but held his fire, concerned about wasting ammunition. He simply hung on tightly to his quarry, who wove in desperate zigzags to evade the fighter. The bomber's rear gunner was silent, apparently wounded. In its panic the Dornier dropped to tree-top height, trying to land in a field. A short burst from the Hurricane: the bomber crashed and burst into flame. Thus the third German that day perished at Urbanowicz's hands within the space of a few minutes, bringing his total to seventeen.

A few days later 303 Squadron moved to a more distant airfield for some R and R.[1] The British, full of admiration for Urbanowicz and not wanting to lose him for even a short time, posted him to Group HQ.

There is no doubt that Urbanowicz represents the evolving new warrior. With honest soldierly ardour he is absorbing the properties of metal, creating a new, healthy, strong, winning alloy, but one not devoid of human characteristics. Aluminium with a nervous system in which beats a living human heart. That is why Urbanowicz was such an interesting type of modern technological man, and perhaps why the British, sensing this, were so keen to court him.

Not just Englishmen, though. Englishwomen too.

---

[1] This was RAF Leconfield where 303 Squadron arrived on the 11th of October 1940. It remained there until the 3rd of January 1941, when it returned to RAF Northolt. Polish Editor's note.

CHAPTER 16

The Myth of the Messerschmitt 110

DURING THE first months of the war, the Germans artfully managed their propaganda to plant successfully in the minds of the frightened world (and the no less dismayed Allies) the notion that they held in reserve a terrible surprise for their enemies in the form of a new 'super-aircraft,' the height of technology, a machine among machines. Something like the Messerschmitt 109, but able to fly higher and faster, and with so powerful an armament that it could destroy every opponent and remain itself essentially indestructible.

Few of these aircraft appeared in the Polish campaign of September 1939, and they were equally rare over France in the spring of 1940. So the Allies had been unable to take its measure. They knew only that this Messerschmitt 110—for that is what the dangerous new beast was called—was a heavily armed twin-engine fighter, with a rear gunner.

However, in the Battle of Britain the Luftwaffe deployed a larger number of Messerschmitt 110s. Then the veil of secrecy was lifted. And it turned out that the beast did not live up to the German boasts. Especially after the rear gunner had been neutralised, which was surprisingly easy to do, the devil could be caught by his horns and pinned to the ground. And finally, on a certain day in September its reputation was shattered, and the myth burst like a soap bubble.

On that day over East Sussex, 303 Squadron met a formation of thirty enemy bombers, Heinkel 111s, heading for London, accompanied by a heavy screen of Messerschmitt 109s. The lead Polish sections attacked the bombers, but seventy or so Messerschmitts zoomed down onto the Hurricanes, plunging the Poles into a furious battle for survival. Fortunately, other British squadrons arrived and their combined efforts held off the enemy.

Urbanowicz, who that day was leading 303 Squadron's rear section, was attacked simultaneously by several Messerschmitts. He managed to dodge death again and again, banking, twisting, turning. When he levelled off he found himself alone, some distance away from the turmoil. On one side he saw the German formation from which he had just successfully escaped, now being attacked by new British fighters. On the other side, about 2,000 yards to the west, he saw an astonishing sight: a long, endless stream of aircraft flying in single file towards London from the south.

Another enemy formation, flying parallel to the first one! All two-engine aircraft, their profiles at a distance reminding Urbanowicz of dive-bombers. But on drawing closer, the fighter pilot realised that they were all Messerschmitt 110s. More than forty of them. Clearly their role was to draw off the British fighters, thereby enabling the formation of Heinkels to break through to London.

Several British fighters flew up to join Urbanowicz; together they launched a joint attack against the head of the enemy line. Instead of fighting, the chain of Messerschmitt 110s immediately turned to port and curled into a tight circle.

The Germans all circled at the same altitude, creating a huge aerial fortress with such heavy all-round firepower that it was impossible to draw near.

Urbanowicz and the British fighters prowled overhead looking in vain for a weak spot. Some tried jabbing at the ring with short bursts and a quick retreat. No success. Two British Hurricanes were already hurtling towards earth in a trail of smoke. Meanwhile the ring continued to rotate—untouched, calm, provocative. In its conceited self-confidence, it was the perfect picture of German arrogance, a wheel of insolence taunting the British skies.

Urbanowicz soon realised that this erratic pecking at the enemy was pointless. Meanwhile, more British fighters had arrived; there were now almost twenty of them. The Pole opened his throttle and waggled his wings. Five other fighters responded and joined him. Plunging out of the sun as a group, they dived on the nearest sector of the ring, to such good effect that three Messerschmitts were knocked out of the circle. They immediately fell within reach of other Hurricanes. Two of the Germans were shot down on the spot. The third fled with two Spitfires on his tail.

The six attacking Hurricanes broke up. Urbanowicz again climbed above the enemy's ring, eager to organise a second attack. He did not get the chance: two Messerschmitt 109s, diving to rescue their comrades, fell on him.

Suddenly, the Pole saw the yellow noses aimed straight at him and a hostile swarm of bluish tracks. With a violent turn, he managed to elude death. So violent was the manoeuvre that he almost blacked out. His mind was still keenly conscious of danger—but his eyes were sightless, his head flopped weakly. The terrible sense of powerlessness at that critical moment

Witold Urbanowicz standing
in front of a Hurricane.

Messerschmitt 110 twin-engine heavy fighters, armed with four machine guns and two cannons in the nose and a rear-facing machine gun in the cockpit area.

303 Squadron Hurricanes race skywards.

Photographed from a German aircraft—an RAF Spitfire blasts past.

Spitfire IIA P7962 RF-A, in which Zumbach was shot down on the 9th of May 1941 over the English Channel.

of battle was a nightmare which would haunt the fighter pilot for the rest of his life...

A moment later, Urbanowicz regained his sight. He spotted a Messerschmitt about 1,800 feet below, but only one. The other had disappeared. The Messerschmitt had pulled out of its dive and was streaking upward. Instantly, Urbanowicz seized this perfect opportunity: throttle, spurt, red light on his gun-sights, press with his thumb; the German banked; press again, again the German banked—then spiralled to earth. That is how it was. Only a few seconds before, the enemy had been a living, strong man, confident of victory. Now he lay motionless and broken on the ground. He had simply ceased to exist, his body smashed into a thousand pieces. In such incalculable leaps from the peaks of existence to nothingness, airmen experience a kind of demonic greatness, a terrifying grandeur...

Again Urbanowicz climbed. He returned to the ring of Messerschmitts. During his absence, there had been changes. In the ring, which continued to circle in the same place, a number of aircraft were trailing smoke. Since they were still in the line but flying more slowly than the others, they left gaps ahead of them. This boded ill for the enemy. His ring was no longer unbroken. Its cohesion was cracking. The Hurricanes were beginning to snap more brashly at its heels. Sometimes too brashly. Urbanowicz saw a British pilot who had come too close: his plane was shot down, and he had baled out. But this did not affect the overall drama. More Hurricanes were arriving, their hoop around the Messerschmitt 110s was growing stronger. Every minute weighted the scales more heavily against the Germans.

One of the German pilots cracked, although still unscathed; with a sudden twist he broke out of the ring and fled towards France—straight into the arms of Urbanowicz. Two Hurricanes were chasing the Messerschmitt. Urbanowicz, being closer, threw himself between the German and the Hurricanes to prevent them from firing. He attacked: one burst from the rear and above. Another after climbing out of his dive. Taking care all the while to cut off the other Hurricanes: this was his prey!

Suddenly the Messerschmitt turned to fight. Urbanowicz zoomed up, flipped over, and raked the German's port engine and cockpit with fire. The Messerschmitt dived to tree-top height. Urbanowicz's fourth attack sent him crashing into the ground, in full view of the two stubborn Hurricanes tenaciously waiting for fortune to smile on them. She did not; they garnered no plunder. The Pole had dealt with the enemy by himself.

When the three Hurricanes returned to the ring they found only half the number of Messerschmitts, about twenty, with several trailing smoke. The Germans continued to circle as if demented. The others, knocked out of the ring and shot down, now littered the ground below. The Messerschmitt 110s had not only failed to accomplish their task of diverting attention from the bomber formation (which had meanwhile been broken up), they had themselves fallen into a lethal trap.

Neither the twin engines nor the rear gunner had made any difference. Arrogant pride had turned into disaster and defeat. There came a moment when the entire ring—that fickle ring of fortune—collapsed like a rotten tree stump. The rest of the Messerschmitts were hunted down as easily as rabbits. A jolly chase began, a brisk rout ensued. This eager hunt fully and finally punctured the inglorious myth of the Messerschmitt 110.

At the heart of Europe an ominous mountain of ravenous steel and powerful myths has risen like a destructive volcano. The aim of this war is to level this mountain, to throttle its ravenousness, to crumble its steel and dispel its myths. History will judge the war's progress by the periods in which myths of all kinds are exploded. One of the first to go was the myth of the Messerschmitt 110.

CHAPTER 17

Tricks

THIS WAR has a monstrous aspect: brutal barbarism has seized control of the finest fruits of science and technology. The Messerschmitt 109 is indeed a technological marvel and a fine testament to human inventiveness. But the skies witness an extraordinary contradiction as well as a grim symbol: when the technological miracle fails, the Messerschmitt pilot, faced with death, reverts to stone-age and jungle. He reaches for the ancient warrior's trusty arsenal: at such moments, the native craftiness of primitive man replaces the refined achievements of military technology.

A Messerschmitt 109 tried to attack the leader of a 303 Squadron section, Lieutenant Henneberg, from above and behind, but broke off when he spotted Second Lieutenant Jan Zumbach coming to the rescue. The German simply passed over the Poles and then, before their very noses, made a wide turn as though taking a cheekily arrogant look at them. Confident in the advantage of his altitude and counting on the presence of other Messerschmitts, he was overconfident, and he underestimated the Poles' guns.

Zumbach pulled up a fraction. He fired off a burst of rounds ahead of the Messerschmitt at a range of about 250 yards, correcting extensively for drift. Zumbach got it right. The German flew through a field of death. He began to smoke and immediately, like a hit partridge, dropped towards the ground. He corkscrewed helplessly down, a victim of his own carelessness.

'Good luck!' Zumbach thought with amusement, and ticked off in his mind his fifth kill that week.

Just as Zumbach was joining his flight leader, he glanced back at his tumbling enemy... and froze. Zumbach is a fighter ace, but he also has a fiery and combustible nature; he now cursed foully. Three thousand feet below, his supposedly beaten adversary had pulled out of his corkscrew dive and was now flying normally in a straight line, heading for France at all possible speed. He wasn't even smoking.

'A joker.' The Pole's voice had an ominous tenderness. Diving, Zumbach accelerated furiously and quickly overtook the fleeing Messerschmitt. When the German caught sight of his pursuer, he again fell into a spin. An incorrigible lover of corkscrew dives!

But this time Zumbach was not fooled. The Hurricane stuck solidly to the Messerschmitt's tail, spiralling down behind him, raking him with fire every other moment. However, Zumbach's rounds were not finding their target—to hit a plane in a corkscrew dive is sheer luck!—and he was firing in mounting anger. In this fashion they dropped from 18,000 feet to 10,000 feet.

Suddenly, Zumbach came to his senses: what madness! If he went on like this, he could use up all his ammunition without hitting the German; indeed, quite the opposite—he could himself become the prey. His opponent's apparently simple manoeuvre was in reality a treacherous trap.

So Zumbach ceased firing. Tenaciously he followed the Messerschmitt, like a silent shadow, watching him. By now Zumbach was quite calm. He knew that the German had no way to escape: either he had to pull out of the dive, or hit the ground. Since he would surely pull out...

It was a sunny day, but occasional clumps of clouds floated like white islands at various altitudes. There were also smaller clouds hanging several hundred feet above the ground. As Zumbach and his opponent dropped past them, the Messerschmitt banked violently and pulled sharply out of his dive. Was this another trick? Was he clutching at safety in these clouds? No-one will ever know.

As soon as the Messerschmitt levelled off, Zumbach's guns opened up. The German unexpectedly rolled—an astonishing and pointless manoeuvre, often used by the Luftwaffe in moments of danger—so that the Pole had to pull up instantly to avoid a collision. He did a sharp back loop and again slanted into German's tail. The black cross neither evaded nor fought. Zumbach fired a few more bursts and finished him off, methodically and simply, like killing a mad dog.

Ablaze, the Messerschmitt now went down for real, no tricks and no pretending.

This is a small cameo in a gigantic war, a minor episode, of which there are legions. The Messerschmitt's deviousness had not saved him. His trick had failed.

When the time comes to pay for the terrible crimes of barbarity and cruelty committed during this war, will the criminals try to avoid responsibility by some new subterfuge? Will there be eyes wise enough and penetrating enough to see through their tricks? More than one pilot from 303 Squadron has wondered.

They are wonderful boys, the lads from 303 'Kościuszko' Squadron, the Warsaw Squadron, healthy, fit, strong, handsome. No surprise that the girls flock to them. For the news is getting around: they are not only victorious fighter pilots, not only exotic defenders of the British homeland, but also amazing fellows, with a great eye for the ladies. The enchanted girls from the Northolt pub, The Orchard, know it, as also do the elegant ladies from the Berkeley or the Dorchester hotels in London.

The wealthy Mrs. Jean Smith-Bingham, the Polish squadron's 'godmother,' held a cocktail party for the fighter pilots at the Dorchester. She invited some of the most beautiful ladies of London society. They came, bright, noble blossoms to meet the famous airmen. They danced together, smiled at one another, drank, made merry, were happy, and fell a little in love. Not that love which is as weighty as fate, but love which is like a brilliant butterfly.

'Capital dancers! Now I know why the gels like 'em!' remarked the portly Marquis of Donegal with an approving sportsman's eye. And although he said that he understood, if the truth be told, he did not really understand the heart of the matter.

After a few drinks, one of the charming ladies, a young widow, lost her English reserve and set her cap at Jan

Zumbach. She whispered sweet nothings to him, marvelled at his broad Polish shoulders, and told him cheerfully:

'I like you, Jan!'

And Zumbach's eyes smiled like a wolf's, for he was the biggest ladies' man of them all. He whispered:

'I love you, too!'

But then something spoiled the English idyll. Zumbach was to blame. Out of the blue he got cold feet. He had clearly drunk too much: he had seen something. Some apparition in the mist, some distant memory. He could see some other eyes the colour of cornflowers. He could see some other lips the colour of cherries. It was not his English lady; it was Zosia. Or maybe Jadzia, or Marysia, although probably Zosia. And he could hear, as clear as a bell, her distant voice, full of tenderness and longing:

'Do you remember me, Jaś?'

When the fighter pilot heard her voice and could suddenly see her with his heart's eyes, his ardour cooled. Nothing in the world would now induce him to tell his beautiful English lady boldly, 'I love you.'

For a heart, a Polish heart, is a strange thing: it can travel the world, it can collapse at forks in the road, don an armour of forgetfulness, become intoxicated with the beauty of a foreign sky—until suddenly and cunningly, it sets up its own trick and falls into its own net. Just to see a smiling Zosia in the distance, or an inviting thatch roof, or a solitary pine in Mazovia in Central Poland. This is a different trick from the one pulled by the enemy in the Messerschmitt, or from other tricks pulled by enemy blackguards: this is an honest, wistful and honourable trick—a trick of the human heart.

Flying Party: Mrs. Arthur Smith-Bingham Entertains the Officers of a Polish Squadron

Out in the country Mrs. Arthur Smith-Bingham has adopted a Polish Squadron of the R.A.F., and keeps open house for them at her home, which is now the lodge instead of the big house of her and her husband's country place. Struggling with the complexities of the English language, the Poles have found a nice, simple name for her: they just call her "Maman." A week or so ago she gave a big party for her "children" in London, and invited all her women friends to help entertain the Polish airmen at the Dorchester. No names can be given for the Polish guests, as the information that they are fighting in Britain might harm their families still in Poland. The party, one of the gayest and most amusing that London has seen for many months, began with dinner, went on with dancing, and included "horse racing" with the girls from the Café de Paris cabaret

Photographs by Swaebe

Lady Stanley of Alderley was one of Mrs. Smith-Bingham's "sub-hostesses" who helped entertain the Polish airmen

Viscountess Elveden, whose husband is in an anti-tank regiment, sat next an officer who had been decorated for valour

A young flying-officer sat between Lady Patricia Gordon-Lennox, Lady Elveden's sister-in-law, and Mrs. Weir

Lady Willoughby de Broke, who flew over most of pre-war Europe with her husband, made easy conversation with her airmen neighbours

Mrs. Douglas Foster, a pilot-officer and Lady Brougham and Vaux were another trio of guests. Lady Brougham and Vaux's husband is in the Army

Another Polish pilot-officer sat beside Miss Elizabeth Profumo, and opposite them at the long table was the Countess of Jersey

FLYING PARTY: MRS. ARTHUR SMITH-BINGHAM ENTERTAINS
THE OFFICERS OF A POLISH SQUADRON

Out in the country Mrs. Arthur Smith-Bingham has adopted a Polish Squadron of the R.A.F., and keeps open house for them at her home, which is now the lodge instead of the big house of her and her husband's country place. Struggling with the complexities of the English language, the Poles have found a nice, simple

Continued overleaf

THE TATLER
AND BYSTANDER
MARCH 5, 1941

Left : Mrs. E. O. Bickford was a " sub-hostess." She is the widow of the late Com. Bickford, D.S.O., R.N., of the Salmon, was Valerie Courtney before her wedding last May

Right : Mrs. Sebastian de Mier, sitting next a Polish pilot-officer, is herself the wife of the only Mexican pilot-officer in the R.A.F. She was Mrs. Eve Richardson

Left : Lady Orr-Lewis helped entertain. She married Sir Duncan Orr-Lewis last year, was Mrs. Phyllis Allan

Right : Mrs. Carol Gibbons, F./O.W. Wittels, and Mrs. Bernard Rubin were neighbours. Mrs. Gibbons' husband came along later to help with the party

Below : Mrs. Arthur Smith-Bingham sits with her grouped guests. How much the Poles appreciate their " Maman " was charmingly demonstrated when they plotted that Mrs. Smith - Bingham should win the " ladies' race " on the Café de Paris hobby-horses

Continued

name for her: they just call her 'Maman.' A week or so ago she gave a big party for her 'children' in London, and invited all her women friends to help entertain the Polish airmen at the Dorchester. No names can be given for the Polish guests, as the information that they are fighting in Britain might harm their families still in Poland. The party, one of the gayest and most amusing that London has seen for many months, began with dinner, went on with dancing, and included 'horse racing' with the girls from the Café de Paris cabaret.

This cocktail party took place long ago, during the memorable days of the Battle of Britain when 303 Squadron from RAF Northolt was defending London with its wings. Much has changed since then in the squadron's composition; most of those fine young airmen have been killed. But Zumbach survived. He took part in all the offensives in the West and suffered not a scratch. Only sometimes he had a curious vision: when he was taking off, in his heart he could see for a moment some girl's eyes. He did not know whose they were, Zosia's, or maybe Wandzia's, or Stasia's.

One could laugh at harmless superstitions and faith in talismans, but there must have been something in those Polish girl's stubborn and good-natured eyes, something which bravely and almost miraculously protected Jan Zumbach, since neither enemy rounds nor other evil consequences of the war affected him.

CHAPTER 18

15th September: Fate in the Balance

THE ENGLISH September of 1940 was unusually sunny and warm. The sky beamed with azure benevolence. The days dawned as if smiling. That decisive Sunday, the 15th, was just such a day: when dawn dissipated the morning mist, low, light clouds appeared in the sky. They swam all day like white swans, while the sun, reflecting from them, shone on England more brightly than ever. So pleasant and enchanting a day—it was difficult to imagine that against such a bucolic backdrop mankind's most critical drama was being played out, that such ethereal colours framed a menacing picture of desperate struggle and its violent consequences.

On that day, the German High Command resolved to settle the outcome of the war.

The air attack on England had already lasted six weeks. Seventy large daylight raids had beat ceaselessly against major British centres of resistance. To be sure, the Luftwaffe had suffered significant losses, losing about 1,650 aircraft, but it was confident that it had inflicted even heavier losses on the British. The Germans had no doubt that the RAF was on its last legs, and that the demoralised British people were on the threshold of revolution. That was one of the Germans' disastrous miscalculations in this war. They were buoyed by wishful thinking and blind arrogance.

While the Germans had wrongly assessed their enemy's situation, they knew very well their own strength: 200 victorious and unstoppable full-strength divisions, which had hitherto crushed every opponent and every obstacle, impatiently awaited the signal to begin the invasion. Tightly clustered on the French shores of the English Channel, they burned with the desire for new conquest. The assault troops, already loaded onto barges, greedily eyed the white cliffs of Kent, awaiting the first breaches to be made by the Luftwaffe. Everything, the fate of that day and of the war, hung on this breach and on the success of the pilots with the black crosses.

It is impossible to establish accurately how many aircraft the Luftwaffe deployed against England that day. Some estimate more than a thousand, but that is surely an exaggeration. It was probably somewhere between 650 and 700. They came in several waves, the two strongest were at noon and three hours later.

The first Messerschmitts appeared in the sky shortly after 09:00 hrs., stretching in a great arc from the north shore of the Thames Estuary to Dungeness in south Kent. These were moderately strong raids, probably intended to gauge the British defence, lure the British into the air, and mislead them. But Fighter Command HQ quickly guessed the German plan, and refused to be drawn into the air.

Suddenly, around 11:00 hrs., a large number of single-engine and twin-engine Messerschmitts appeared. They flew very high and at full throttle, leaving white contrails in their wake. Those white streaks—by now a common sight over the valleys of Kent—were unmistakable in their menace. They cut the sky like enemy arrows aimed at a single heart: London.

Although this was now a major raid of several German squadrons, British Fighter Command offered only token resistance, allowing the Germans to penetrate inland. Fighter Command intentionally let the Germans through: a most appropriate decision that favourably influenced subsequent events.

The battle, which began a few minutes later, again proved the courage and skill of the British and Allied fighter pilots, and also demonstrated the expertise of RAF Fighter Command. A week earlier, on the 7th of September, its staff work had failed, for the Germans had slipped through to the London docks in broad daylight. Now, however, a clear, watchful and decisive hand was at the wheel. Not for one moment did the British lose the initiative. Their superb system of radio intercepts and direction-finding provided them with accurate information on the enemy. All enemy formations were continuously charted on their plotting table. They fed RAF fighter squadrons into the battle one after another, wisely, thoughtfully and accurately. They had a clear plan of defence; every new turn of the battle was immediately countered, with success. Somewhere in England, in the Fighter Command operations room deep underground, for half an hour the entire energy of Britain seemed focused on infusing the wings of its fighter squadrons with the will to victory.

A few minutes after the advance guard of German fighters had flown further inland, a new roar of engines, deeper and more penetrating, was heard near Dover. A powerful formation spanned the sky from the east: about forty bombers, mainly Heinkels, escorted by double that number of Messerschmitts. Immediately after the German formation crossed the coast, two or three squadrons of Spitfires hurled themselves at it. They pounced upon the Germans like ferocious hounds. Their attack was so violent that it achieved the mission assigned by the British commanders: the Spitfires engaged most of the Messerschmitts, and the bombers flew on with a much reduced fighter cover.

About twenty-five miles further inland, half-way between London and the coast, the bombers hit a new, stronger barrier of Hurricanes, forming the second and main line of defence. Here the Luftwaffe's momentum evaporated. The bomber formation, forced to fight, scattered. Thus it ceased to exist as a strike force. The formation disintegrated into several dozen individual duels, and was defeated.

However, the Heinkels were but the opening act of the day's drama.

Barely five minutes later, a new and much larger formation arrived: about 150 German aircraft, more than a third of them bombers. They struck England like a mighty hammer. Only now had the decisive moment arrived.

A very real and urgent danger hung over the country. The preceding German waves had been sent only to fight, engage and wear down the British defence (in the opinion of the German High Command, already gravely weakened by the six weeks' fighting). This new raid would achieve final control of the skies over England. If only for a short time, an hour or two: just long enough to create an opening for the next waves of the invasion.

Like a raging storm, the huge raid crossed the coast unopposed. There were Spitfires in the air, but they were still fighting the Messerschmitts. The storm headed straight for London. Over Maidstone it entered the sector where a massive battle between the earlier raid and defending Hurricanes sprawled over a number of miles. The German armada skirted that fight, and continued on its course. It was almost clear of the battle zone, when suddenly, to the invaders' astonishment, fresh British fighter squadrons rose to challenge them. It was a painful shock to the Germans. But the raid had such a powerful momentum, that even though the British struck fatal daggers into its ranks, they succeeded in stopping and engaging only about half of the raiders; the rest flew on.

The raid reached London. The Germans roared over London just as Big Ben was solemnly striking noon. There were a great many bombers among them, but they failed to cause much damage. They did not have the chance. For at that moment the Germans were met by several new fighter squadrons called up from other parts of England. These formed a third and final line of defence. Under their desperate blows the German formations shattered. Broken up, caught in scores of individual dogfights, the Germans turned and fled.

The storm was over. British Fighter Command had won. It had broken up the enemy's formations. Its fighter pilots finished the job. On a broad stretch of sky from London to the Channel coast raged the most unusual battle in the annals of warfare. Two hundred fierce dogfights: a sight of indescribable beauty and menacing turmoil. The British and Allied pilots knew why they were fighting, and they fought like lions.

No-one knows what might have happened if in those dozen or so minutes a fresh new enemy wave had appeared— probably disaster. Twenty-one British fighter squadrons were already engaged. There were clearly few reserves close to hand, since earlier squadrons had been called up from further afield. But the German High Command did not mount a new attack. It cringed and froze, probably stunned by the unexpectedly strong defence which had ruined its plans.

John Kent

From the left: Henneberg, Kent and Pisarek.

From the left: Kent, Żak and Łokuciewski.

So, starved of new fuel, the great flame over England began to burn out. Its waning fire brought success to the British.

303 Squadron fought magnificently in this crucial battle. It covered itself with new glory, although initially things did not go too well.

That day 303 Squadron was led by the Canadian, Flight Lieutenant John Kent, a brave fighter pilot, but young and still inexperienced. Kent, at the head of twelve aircraft, saw over Tonbridge a group of some twenty Messerschmitts flying towards London. Tempted by the attractive target, he set off in pursuit with his squadron. Unfortunately, the Messerschmitts were fast and difficult to catch. But Kent spurred ahead, continuing the chase. The Messerschmitts turned slightly north, leading the squadron over the Thames Estuary, and then traced a large circle, returning to the Tonbridge area.

Led a pretty dance, the squadron not only squandered a dozen or so valuable minutes, but, much worse, the prolonged chase had scattered its formation, its own sections losing contact with each other as well as the enemy. When it returned to the combat zone, the squadron had broken up into four separate groups of three. This put it at a terrible disadvantage, and yet in just such difficult circumstances the Polish pilots of 303 Squadron once again demonstrated their superb skills as individual fighters.

The first section, Kent's, having flown as far as Dungeness on the coast, brashly attacked a dozen or so Messerschmitts. Kent's two wingmen, Second Lieutenant Ferić and Sergeant Andruszków, bagged two Germans in the middle of the formation, then saved themselves from certain doom by a desperate plunge into the clouds. They escaped unscathed.

The second section, Lieutenant Henneberg's, was attacked by Messerschmitts as it was speeding toward a formation of Dorniers. The Polish pilots scattered. This is when Zumbach downed the 'tricky' Messerschmitt, who evaded with corkscrew dives. Meanwhile, Henneberg single-handedly hunted the Dorniers, which flew with a strong fighter escort. With one long burst, he set afire the first Dornier, eluded the onrushing Messerschmitts with a daring dive under the bombers, then attacked four new Messerschmitts, downing one of them. He got away in one piece.

The third section, led by Lieutenant Paszkiewicz, was jumped by a number of Messerschmitts. Instantly the Poles split up. Paszkiewicz engaged one of his attackers in a dog-fight, and soon shot him down. Meanwhile, Second Lieutenant 'Tolo' Łokuciewski, escaping, noticed a lone Messerschmitt off to one side, flying slowly. It turned out to be a decoy. As Tolo drew near, firing off a few rounds, several Messerschmitts fell on him from above. One of their rounds shattered the side of his cockpit and wounded him badly. Tolo saved his life with a lightning dart into the clouds. But before disappearing, he had the satisfaction of seeing the decoy Messerschmitt falling from the sky in flames. Apparently his short burst had found its mark. Although his Hurricane was badly shot up and he had innumerable splinters in his thigh, Tolo, the indomitable fighter pilot, brought his aircraft home, to put the Hurricane into the repair shop and himself in hospital.

The leader of the fourth section, Lieutenant Marian Pisarek, had alongside him Sergeant František who, up to his old tricks, peeled off in order to shoot down a Messerschmitt 110 somewhere over the Channel. Pisarek began to chase a Messerschmitt 109, which neatly avoided his fire by clever evasive manoeuvres. The 'little Adolf,' quite adept at his game, finally sneaked into a small cloud. Pisarek followed him in, but immediately lost sight of his quarry. Once in cover, the German abandoned his clever games; he probably felt safe and turned towards France. Pisarek, instinctively reading his mind, did the same. When the Pole shot out of the cloud, he had the Messerschmitt right in front of him. His first burst of fire easily downed the German. In this game of hide-and-seek, both opponents had had the same idea—and the enemy paid with his life.

Thus 303 Squadron, although scattered, did very well. With its audacious bravery—both audacity and bravery being the most essential attributes that day—it tied up a large number of Messerschmitts, allowing other squadrons to deal with the bombers. And, last but not least, it set a new record for victories: although 303 Squadron was only one of twenty-one British squadrons (less than 5 percent of the total), all pushing themselves to the limit, it destroyed almost one-sixth (almost 16 percent) of all the enemy aircraft shot down in that mid-day attack: nine and a half (half, because it shared one Messerschmitt with another squadron) out of a total of sixty and a half enemy aircraft destroyed. A distinguished result.

The British losses were negligible: a dozen or so aircraft and only a few killed. 303 Squadron's losses: one wounded.

Winston Churchill, together with his wife, had been following the course of the battle at 11 Group Headquarters at RAF Uxbridge. He had wanted to light up one of his legendary cigars, but was tactfully asked not to smoke in the operations room. Therefore, an unlit cigar was clamped in his mouth when the tension of battle reached its climax. The Prime Minister left Uxbridge only after four o'clock in the afternoon when, on that most critical day in the Battle of Britain, the British had handed the German Luftwaffe a clear and shattering defeat. Pleased and smiling, Churchill thanked the airmen: the British fighter pilots and their Allies had accomplished their task.

The great page of history had turned in favour of the British, and in favour of the whole of mankind.

It will be a source of honest pride to Poles for all times that Polish names are clearly written on this page, and in some of its most important lines. In addition to 303 Squadron, another Polish squadron, 302 'City of Poznań' Squadron, took part in the epic battles of that day, and also shot down a number of enemy aircraft: eight to be exact.

But the 15th of September was still not over...

CHAPTER 19

15th September: Fate Decided

THE GERMAN barges loaded with assault troops still waited
for the invasion signal. A path had to be cleared for them.
Whatever the cost, England's resistance had to be broken and
its skies controlled. 'The last aircraft *will* be victorious!' raged
Reichsmarschall Göring, commander of the Luftwaffe.

Two hours after the Luftwaffe's mid-day defeat, enemy
engines again roared over the South Coast of England. That
Sunday's second raid was as powerful as the first. Again it
came in two waves, one after the other. The first was by far
the stronger. It was crushing. It traced the most ominous signs
in the sky. Focusing all the desires of the Teutonic Knights,
it carried the Germans' most rapacious hopes. It was like
rolling thunder.

303 Squadron was scrambled at 14:50 hrs. Only nine
Hurricanes were available. Squadron Leader Kellett led the
first flight with four aircraft; Lieutenant Urbanowicz led the
second with five aircraft. After take-off, fighter control ordered
a south-easterly heading and a climb to 20,000 feet.

At an altitude of about 8,000 feet the squadron entered a

dense layer of cloud. Useful perhaps to cover England, but unhelpful to the fighter pilots. It became difficult to maintain contact between the sections. The pilots of the second flight snuggled up close to Urbanowicz's aircraft, like baby chicks to their mother. It was hazardous flying, with a real risk of collision owing to the poor visibility. To make matters worse, windscreens began to freeze over and were soon covered in a thick layer of ice. Nerves began to fray. The possibility of an accident grew greater…

Finally! A long-awaited gleam: the flight soared out of the clouds. Altitude: 22,000 feet. The screen of cloud below, almost 3 miles thick, from above seemed a majestically towering range of mountains.

A complete wilderness. The fighter pilots looked in vain for their comrades from the first flight. They were alone, just the five of them, in this endless sea of white and sunshine. The rest of the squadron was lost in the clouds. There was no-one else to be seen—not a trace of the other fighters, not a trace of the enemy.

The five Hurricanes, like a flock of birds lost in that expanse, flew on along the designated heading, continuing to climb. Ever higher and higher. The ice on the windscreens soon melted in the sun, and the flight could see again.

Suddenly they spotted something! In the distance, about two and a half miles in front of them, small white puffs were bursting in the sky. Anti-aircraft shells, swarming up through the clouds. From a distance, it looked like a child's game, but the fighters were moved by those pugnacious gunners firing blindly, defiantly, despite the thick cloud cover.

At the same time they also saw the gunners' target: a bomber raid. More than sixty of them, in tight columns of five, flying several hundred feet above the clouds towards London.

Urbanowicz took in their compact mass, guessed that they were Dornier 215s. Automatically, anxiously, he scanned the sky for the fighter screen. Where was the screen? There! He spotted the German fighters. Some way behind the bombers, to port, in the sun, but oddly high, unusually high—about 6,000 feet above the Dorniers—flew a powerful formation of approximately one hundred Messerschmitts. They blackened the sky like a fearsome swarm of bees. But why so high? The experienced fighter pilot could not understand it; he noticed a few sections of three Messerschmitts each, circling below the top formation, between it and the bomber force.

Soon Urbanowicz's attention was drawn to five Messerschmitt 110s. Barely 600 yards away, they were flying in the same direction as the Polish flight, but much higher and to one side. Their sudden proximity settled it: Urbanowicz set off in pursuit. But within a dozen or so seconds, he realised the futility of chasing them. Forced to climb, even at full throttle, he was falling behind the Messerschmitts. Urbanowicz abandoned his decision as swiftly as he had taken it. He chose another target: the bombers themselves.

The pursuit of the Messerschmitt 110s had brought the flight within striking distance of the bombers. They were just ahead, to port, several hundred feet below the Poles. And at the same time, almost directly beneath the swarm of Messerschmitts. Urbanowicz glanced up, rigid with tension: not one of the Germans was diving to attack. An extraordinary opportunity! The Messerschmitts were either ignoring the flight—five fighters were a mere drop compared to their superior numbers!—or from their lofty perch they had not yet seen them. A quite fortuitous chain of circumstances had landed the Poles in the middle of the German formation, which was unaware of the danger.

Urbanowicz turned sharply to port. Into the attack. His comrades understood. They too turned, ranged up alongside him. All five plummeted together. In a line. On full throttle. Thundering down. Only eagles attack like that! A mad dash that shaved off seconds: the loose threes of Messerschmitts were still circling above the bombers. To flash through them, beat them to the punch! Meanwhile, Urbanowicz missed nothing: two British fighter squadrons were approaching some 2,000 yards ahead of the bomber formation. In a moment the Polish flight would not be alone. But it would be first.

And first it was. An attack three-quarters from the front and from above. Right out of the sun. Right at the bombers. The bombers huddled together like a flock of sheep. The first rounds were fired at a range of 400 yards. Accurate and shrewd: the Poles did not focus a long burst on a single aircraft, as they usually did; instead they sprayed individual bombers with short bursts. Here they damaged, there they destroyed. One burst, and on to the next target. They raked a dozen bombers almost at once, the whole port flank was in their line of fire. Right in their line of fire! Most effective and demoralising fire.

No-one will know how it happened: whether the accuracy of the Poles' fire caused an exceptionally high casualty rate among the German crews, or whether the German crews were completely unnerved by the unexpected attack out of the sun, where a strong Messerschmitt screen was supposed to be on guard—in any event, the enemy lost his head. The attack devastated him. Panic broke out. Almost immediately, two Dorniers crashed into each other; both plunged from the sky, intertwined in a terrible embrace. Bombers in the outer columns swung frantically to port; some in the centre dived sharply to escape.

Inspection over, this Hurricane is ready to fly.

A pilot straps on his parachute before a combat mission.

Hurricane V6665 RF-J in which Andruszków was killed on the 27th of September 1940.

A 303 Squadron pilot is buried with full honours by his comrades-in-arms.

The five Poles charged in to the attack. Two of them riddled the formation from top to bottom and from bottom to top; the other three remained above the bombers. They swooped and dived, looped the loop, fired from above, flipped over, dived, fired. Looping again, they opened fired from above. Again and again, climbing, diving, firing. They blazed away, hammered again... Thus five fighter pilots, transformed into five raging furies, revelling in their element, made history: they smashed a major Luftwaffe raid.

The raid disintegrated. Nothing could stitch it together again. Panic is a terrible thing. Even the bombers in the starboard column, hitherto the least threatened, were banking and fleeing. They fled—but now fresh British fighter squadrons jumped them, like new furies wreaking new havoc.

Finally the top cover of Messerschmitts attacked. They were too far away, they arrived too late. What matter that Sergeant Brzezowski, riddled by enemy fire, died? That Sergeant Andruszków had his machine shot up and was forced to bale out—and baling out, got hung up on his radio lead, his plunging Hurricane nastily dragging him by the head for half a mile before he broke free by tearing off his helmet? That Second Lieutenant Ferić was pounced on by a swarm of Messerschmitt 110s? In the brawl Ferić took down one of them and then, with his Hurricane damaged, bolted into the clouds.

Messerschmitts were diving in from all sides. But they could not change the course of the battle. They could not save the bombers from destruction. The Hurricanes and Spitfires that rushed to join the mêlée finished the job. And among them was the happy man who had first got to the enemy: Urbanowicz.

At one point, he suddenly spotted three Dorniers, taking advantage of the confusion, diving through a gap in the clouds to get closer to the ground, doubtlessly to unload their bombs. Sneaking off, one after the other. Urbanowicz raced over. He flew around them like a wasp, climbing, diving, stinging. At the second attack, the middle bomber burst into flame. The next burst swept away the lead Dornier. The third one—damn it!—dodged into the clouds. As he prudently disappeared from sight, the other two Dorniers were falling like shot ducks into the middle of the Thames Estuary.

Once again, just as three hours earlier, 200 dogfights raged over the sky. The Germans were being destroyed, their aircraft hurtling to earth.

The Luftwaffe suffered a most crushing defeat. It lost 185 aircraft that day, counting both the morning and the afternoon. Over 200 more, badly damaged, barely limped back to France. It was a decisive blow.

When, on the afternoon of that 15th of September 1940, between the hours of three and three-thirty, the remnants of the shattered Luftwaffe were high-tailing it for France, the great battle, known as the Battle of Britain, was decided.

Few Britons, sitting down that afternoon to their Sunday tea, were aware of the great victory. Even fewer understood that the fate of this second and most dreadful world war had been determined that day.

Never has the world's destiny hung on a single hour as it did on the 15th of September 1940.

CHAPTER 20

'We Are Beginning to Understand the Poles'

THE SECOND half of September showed clearly that the 15th of the month had been the high point of the Battle of Britain—the aerial battles that day had decisively broken the German offensive. The Luftwaffe never rallied after that day. Its raids lost their bite, weakened. If they did occasionally flare up with a final, desperate fire, British and Allied fighters easily drowned them in blood, shattered them into pieces. Thus, for instance, on the 27th of September, the British destroyed 116 German aircraft. 303 Squadron accounted for fifteen. But these were the final flickers.

Great Britain survived. Only those intimately involved knew how close to total disaster they had been during that September of 1940: the country had almost no ground defence.

The battle was won by the fighter pilots. They had prevented the German hordes from invading. On that decisive day, the 15th of September 1940, twenty-one British and Allied squadrons, about 250 fighter pilots, took the full force of the Germans' fury, defending the entire British Empire. Even today, years later, just the memory of it is breathtaking. It seems like some extraordinary accident of history, some miraculous paradox: the destiny of millions dependent on a handful of gallant men...

Thin was the thread holding Great Britain together, but it did not break. And by not breaking, it aroused the world's conscience. Only when, by superhuman effort and bravery these 'few' had accomplished their mission, did the rest of the Empire and the United States waken to the reality of this war.

The front defended by these 250 pilots was at the time miniscule—but oh so important, oh so significant in its effect: it cleared a path to the real front opened later by the entire world. A front that stretched from Washington through London and Moscow, to Chunking. Only an armed force of global dimensions would eventually throttle the Nazi German Hydra. But at the time, in August and September 1940, that global force did not yet exist. There was only a thin, solitary thread. They were very, very few in number.

Among those few were the Poles. And among the Poles was 303 Squadron. Its contribution to the Battle of Britain in its most crucial September phase was magnificent and extraordinary: 303 Squadron shot down three times more enemy aircraft than the average of the other RAF squadrons. Yet its own losses were only one-third those of other squadrons.

In statistical terms, the results of all the Polish fighter pilots in September, as well as those of the RAF, were as follows:

• 303 Squadron: 77 German aircraft destroyed by Polish pilots, 17 by the Czech František and 14 by the squadron's three British members. Altogether, in September, 108 kills, and in the whole Battle of Britain—126.

• 302 Squadron: 15 kills in September, and in the whole Battle of Britain—16.

• Other Polish fighter pilots, scattered throughout British units: 29 kills in September, and in the whole Battle of Britain—77.

Altogether, the Poles in September 1940 notched up 121 German aircraft destroyed; the rest of the RAF—846. Thus during the month of September 1940, the Poles accounted for one out of every eight German aircraft shot down by the RAF. Anti-aircraft artillery brought down another 131 German aircraft during this period.

Even more impressive was the Polish 'kill ratio' on that decisive day, the 15th of September. Together, 303 Squadron (15 kills), 302 Squadron (8 kills), and the other British squadrons with Poles in them notched up a total of 26 German kills. The remaining British and Allied pilots shot down 153 enemy aircraft. In other words, on that critical day every seventh German aircraft was shot down by Polish fire.

No surprise then that the Polish fighter pilots were on the lips and in the hearts of every Briton. No surprise that General Sikorski visited 303 Squadron to award decorations, that the King of England came to shake their hands and thank them. British writers, with even greater honesty, lauded them enthusiastically in the press during the autumn of 1940—an example being Hilary St. George Saunders, the well-known author of a popular little work entitled *The Battle of Britain*:

Conspicuous among them [the fighter pilots] are the Poles. Their valour is tremendous; their skill bordering on the inhuman. They have done great service. They are still doing it, and they will go on doing it until victory, triumphant and complete, lights up their wings. We are beginning to understand the Poles...

So, at the end of the day, what were they like, these famous fighter pilots of 303 Squadron? Were they some kind of supermen? Some kind of élite, selected for public consumption as a national symbol? Golden children, on whom the gods smiled?

No, they were not! They were normal, healthy, down-to-earth fellows. They had the same temperament and the same desires, the same smile and the same worries as most other Poles. They were inch for inch the same as other people from the Vistula, the Warta and the Bug; they were in no way different, either in terms of virtues or vices. They had simply learned their trade well in a Polish school and were now conscientiously doing their duty—that was their secret.

That the effectiveness and accomplishments of the Polish fighter pilots of 303 Squadron in 1940 were not unusual is proved by the fact that other Polish fighter pilots scattered throughout British units achieved similarly outstanding results, as did their comrades in 302 'City of Poznań' Squadron. The pilots of 302 Squadron even set a kind of record: although based further from the front lines, they still managed to shoot down sixteen enemy aircraft during the Battle of Britain. And when, on the 15th of September, they were finally let loose on the enemy, they swept no fewer than eight of his aircraft from the sky.

The story of the Polish airmen in Great Britain is not without its tragic elements, in some ways mirroring the tragedy of Poland itself. Even the most objective of other countries held the oddest, at times outlandish, misconceptions about the Poles. Poland's position was about the worst in the world, sandwiched between two insatiable powers employing the most ruthless propaganda machines. For that reason, information about Poland was often inaccurate and biased.

King George VI, visiting 303 Squadron at RAF Northolt on the 26th of
September 1940, shakes hands with Ferić. Visible in the line-up to the left
of Ferić are Zumbach, Grzeszczak and Januszewicz.

The entire personnel of 303 Squadron photographed at RAF Northolt during
late September or early October 1940.

On the 16th of January 1941, Urbanowicz, Kellett, Kent and Forbes are decorated with the Silver Cross of the Virtuti Militari by General Sikorski.

From the left: Bienkowski and Zumbach with the 303 Squadron trophy—a tail section of a Junkers 88 downed in January 1942. It was the 178th German aircraft destroyed by the squadron.

(One small example was the use in British atlases of German names and terms for Polish towns and places, e.g.: Posen for Poznań, Lemberg for Lwów, 'Polish Corridor' for Pomerania, etc.)

In the summer of 1940, the highest reaches of British Fighter Command, conscious of their great responsibility, harboured doubts as to whether the Polish fighter pilots should be used in the defence of England. They assumed that the Poles, having suffered defeats in Poland and in France, were demoralised and unsuited for combat in such a critical sector. When the Poles were finally assigned, however, it quickly became apparent how mistaken this negative assessment had been.

Later, it was commonly assumed that the Polish fighter pilots were so successful because they were crazy daredevils, holding no regard for their own lives. Not true: far fewer Poles than British lost their lives.

'The Poles are good only as fighter pilots, because of their volatile temperament.' Not true: numerous Polish bomber crews distinguished themselves by the exceptional precision of their work and brave support of their British colleagues.

'The Poles are only a nation of landlubbers!' Not true: look at the spirit inspiring our *Orzełs*, *Błyskawicas* and *Kromańs*,[1] or examine the forceful and robust contributions of the Polish merchant marine.

Enough of these lists!

The Germans had always declared (and the world was inclined to believe them) that the Poles were an ungovernable lot, incapable of creative work and organized effort. But within ten years of Poland regaining its independence as a

---

[1] The first two were Polish warships and the third a Polish merchant vessel. In each case, the final 's' is an English plural. Translator's note.

nation (after 123 years of partition by Germany, Austria and Russia), the small fishing village of Gdynia grew into the largest port on the Baltic, with a turnover greater than that of Stettin, Stockholm or Leningrad; in the south of Poland, a new Central Industrial Region was developing at a remarkable rate, until the Germans invaded.

Poland's other near neighbour, the Soviet Union, had for years been telling the world that the Poles were a nation of reactionary landlords and romantic arrogant aristocrats. Yet Poland's social and labour legislation was perhaps the most liberal and comprehensive in Europe.

A nation of aristocrats—yet nearly all the Polish airmen fighting in Britain are sons of the middle and labouring classes.

If the Polish airmen were ever asked how much Great Britain owed them for their contribution to the war and how it should repay them—a blunt, but honest, question—the airmen would have opened wide their eyes and bridled, perhaps somewhat offended: they were simply doing their duty as loyal allies against a common enemy; they expected no payment from Britain.

But later, after thinking it over, they might have asked for something. Namely, they would have asked the British and others to get to know the Poles better. To get to know them honestly, sincerely and well, without prejudice: to get to know them as they really are and not as they are often portrayed, distorted and wooden.

Then the British would surely discover that the people living on the Vistula and the Warta are just the same as all other mature and civilised nations, neither better nor worse. That the average Pole is no different from the average Mr. Brown in London, or Mr. Bruce in Edinburgh, or Mr. Taylor in Chicago. That he, just as they, believes in the existence of great human moral values—and that he will neither break his word, nor give birth to Quislings.[2]

That is the payment the Polish airmen would have demanded: a fair and sensible appraisal of the Poles.

---

[2] The term 'Quisling' denotes a traitor, particularly one who collaborates with the enemy. It derives from the name of Vidkun Quisling, an infamous Norwegian who collaborated with Nazi Germany during World War II, heading the puppet government installed by the Germans in Norway after they invaded that country in April 1940. Following the war's end in May 1945, the legitimate Norwegian government tried Quisling for high treason. He was convicted, and was executed by firing squad on the 24th of October 1945. Translator's note.

HISTORICAL HORIZON

THE ROAD TO BRITAIN

FOR THE POLISH AIR FORCE:

A BRIEF OVERVIEW

The British, French and Polish Alliance, 1939

International tensions mounted steadily during the spring and summer of 1939. Over the preceding four years, Nazi Germany had rearmed in contravention of the Treaty of Versailles that ended World War I, and had begun taking over neighbouring territories.

In March 1939, Germany ignored its promises to Great Britain and France in the Munich Agreement of only six months before, and occupied the remaining portions of Czechoslovakia.[1] Poland was clearly next in its sights. Germany was threatening to seize the Baltic port of Danzig (Gdańsk), designated as a 'free city' under the Treaty of Versailles, which would have jeopardised Poland's access to the sea. Great Britain and France pledged to support Poland in the event of hostilities.

The announcement of the Molotov–Ribbentrop Pact, the non-aggression treaty signed 23 August 1939 by Germany and the Soviet Union, shocked the rest of Europe—as late as 21 August, Britain and France had been in negotiations with the Soviet Union for a tripartite alliance against Germany. On 25 August, Great Britain renewed its pledge of support to Poland.

War appeared imminent. Polish forces were mobilised.

---

[1] After signing the Munich Agreement in September 1938, in which Germany promised to go no further after taking over the resource-rich Sudetenland in Czechoslovakia, British Prime Minister Neville Chamberlain had returned to Great Britain announcing 'peace for our time.'

The Polish Defensive Campaign, September 1939

Germany invaded Poland on 1 September 1939. From the first day, the German Luftwaffe sent waves of bombers and fighters to ravage Poland. On 3 September, Britain and France honoured their pacts with Poland and declared war on Germany. World War II had begun.

Because all operational units of the Polish Air Force had been moved to forward airfields at the end of August, they escaped destruction in the initial German attacks. But the Germans rapidly achieved air supremacy over Poland. The Luftwaffe had a numerical advantage of at least four to one in all aircraft, with a ratio of at least nine to one in fighter aircraft. German fighter aircraft were also significantly superior in performance and armament.

Facing overwhelming odds, the Polish fighter pilots drew on their personal strengths: a strong fighting spirit, high morale, superb aerial skills, determination and courage. They made up for lack of speed by attacking head on, and for weaker armament by holding fire until at point-blank range. Such tactics, born out of necessity, later gave them a distinct advantage when they flew the more powerful and better-equipped Hurricanes during the Battle of Britain.

Polish bomber squadrons, ordered to concentrate on close support of their ground forces, fought bravely, but sustained extremely heavy losses from flak and German fighters.

Polish Air Force operations were hampered by poor communications and inadequate logistical support. Spare parts, repair facilities and fuel were in short supply, resulting in a severe shortage of serviceable aircraft. There were continuous changes of airfields and landing grounds; pilots,

By late August 1939, war appears imminent. Poland begins to mobilise its armed forces.

On 1 September 1939, Germany invades Poland. A week later, German forces are at the outskirts of Warsaw, the Polish capital.

Polish P. 11 fighters at a forward airfield in south-east Poland. All prominent emblems are over-painted and the aircraft are heavily camouflaged while on the ground to protect them from German attack.

A Polish P. 7 fighter on patrol.

The burning wreckage of a downed Polish P. 11.

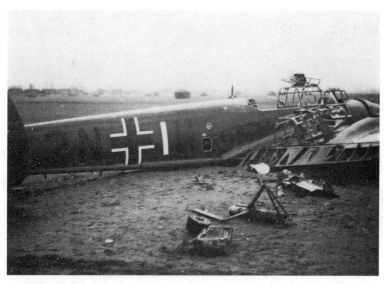

German Messerschmitt 110 downed on 6 September 1939 by Second Lieutenant Wiktor Strzembosz of 111 Eskadra Myśliwska 'Kościuszko.' Strzembosz later flew with 303 Squadron.

Polish bomber crews in front of their P. 37 Łoś bombers.

A P. 37 Łoś bomber destroyed in its hangar.

ground crew and advance parties lost contact with each other; roads were frequently impassable because of masses of civilian refugees fleeing the German attacks.

By the middle of September, about four-fifths of the Polish Air Force, including its HQ and all the Air Force flying schools, had been moved to south-east Poland within two hours' march of the Romanian border. At that time, Romania was neutral. Much-needed aircraft from France and Britain were expected to be delivered by sea to Romanian ports, where they would be unloaded and delivered to the Poles. Romania had agreed to permit the Poles to assemble the aircraft and train their crews while in Romania.

But this plan was never carried out. On 17 September, the Soviet Union invaded Poland from the east. Trapped between two implacable enemies, with no immediately effective military assistance from its British and French allies, Poland's fate was sealed. Polish Air Force HQ ordered its forces in south-east Poland to cross the border.

In the meantime, Polish Air Force detachments in besieged Warsaw continued to fight. They only evacuated their remaining aircraft in late September, under cover of darkness and in the face of heavy German artillery fire, just before the capital surrendered.

Despite the disadvantages under which Polish fighter pilots operated during their few weeks of combat in September 1939, they are credited with the destruction of 126 German aircraft, plus another 10 probably destroyed and 14 damaged. Overall, the Polish Air Force lost approximately 85 percent of all its aircraft from all causes. Estimates of total Luftwaffe losses vary widely, with anywhere from approximately 250 to 600 German aircraft destroyed or damaged from all causes, including those downed by Polish anti-aircraft fire.

Sikorski's Tourists

The Polish campaign was lost—but the Poles did not give up the fight.

The Polish government had evacuated in early September and was re-constituted in France. General Władysław Sikorski became Prime Minister of the Polish government-in-exile and Commander-in-Chief of the Polish Armed Forces, which he immediately began re-forming to fight at the side of their French allies.

At the same time, an underground resistance organisation was being set up within Poland, which would eventually include both an entire civil government and a military structure (the Armia Krajowa—'AK' or Home Army), under the ultimate authority of the government-in-exile.

Most of the Polish airmen and soldiers who escaped from Poland crossed the south-east border into Romania and Hungary. On arrival, the Poles were interned in camps by those countries.

The Polish government-in-exile quickly built up an efficient, large-scale organisation to assist its interned troops in escaping and making their way to France. Escape proved relatively easy in the early weeks, but became more challenging as the Germans and Soviets exerted increasing pressure on neutral countries.

By circuitous routes, often through the Mediterranean and Middle East, travelling individually or in groups, in civilian clothes or uniforms from which military insignia had been removed, Polish airmen and soldiers (nicknamed 'Sikorski's tourists') eventually reached France. Others made it to France via the Baltic states or Scandinavia. By May 1940,

On 17 September 1939, the Soviet Union invades Poland from the east. Caught between two implacable enemies, Poland's fate is sealed.

Some of 'Sikorski's tourists'—this group of Polish Air Force cadet-officers, led by their instructor and the future 303 Squadron OC Witold Urbanowicz (*centre front, wearing a chequered scarf*), reached France in 1940 as a complete unit. Most are dressed in civilian clothes, but some wear Polish uniforms with the military insignia removed.

The main gate of the Lyon-Bron centre, which became the principal establishment of the Polish Air Force while in France from late 1939 to early 1940.

Morane-Saulnier M.S. 406 fighters of the 'Groupe Montpellier,' assembled at the Lyon-Bron aerodrome on 27 March 1940. The Polish national red-and-white 'chequerboard' marking is visible on the aircraft fuselages.

Second Lieutenant Jan Daszewski, future 303 Squadron pilot, by a Curtiss Hawk 75 fighter during his service with the Polish Air Force in France, where he flew with the Défense Aérienne du Territoire at Bourges.

By 27 May 1940, more than 330,000 British and Allied troops were trapped by the Germans on the beaches at Dunkirk. The Royal Navy, aided by some 700 small private British boats and RAF air support, rescued them by 4 June. Here, some of the rescued troops take a last look at the burning French coast.

Bloch M.B. 152 fighter of Lieutenant Zdzisław Henneberg's unit at Châteauroux. After the French collapse in mid-June, Henneberg (a future 303 Squadron pilot) evacuated his unit to Great Britain—the only Polish unit to fly its aircraft out of France.

Airmen with 'POLAND' shoulder patches went on to distinguish themselves in all theatres of Allied operations in Europe. Here, in September 1940 British King George VI personally congratulates the pilots of 303 Squadron on their outstanding record.

more than 8,500 Polish airmen, both pilots and ground crew, had escaped to the West, together with some 30,000 or so Polish soldiers.

In addition to those who had escaped from Poland, the Polish Armed Forces in France recruited approximately 40,000 troops from among ethnic Poles living in France.

The Short-Lived French Campaign

There was every expectation that the Germans would soon be stopped: the French had mobilised an army of some six million men, which was augmented by several hundred thousand troops from Great Britain and the smaller Allies.

In early 1940, the Polish Air Force had entered into an agreement with the French under which Polish fighter squadrons would be formed to fight with the French Air Force.

Despite bureaucratic delays, lack of organisation and various other obstacles, more than 150 Polish fighter pilots[2] did in fact fly combat sorties against the German Luftwaffe during the short-lived Battle of France in May and June 1940. But within a few short weeks, the German Blitzkrieg had toppled France along with the smaller Allies—and the Polish airmen were escaping yet again, this time to England.

Polish Airmen in Great Britain

The Polish Air Force had begun negotiations with the RAF in October 1939, seeking to re-establish the Polish Air Force in Great Britain. The British were reluctant to devote sufficient resources to accommodate the entire Polish Air

---

[2] Approximately 70 percent of the Polish pilots in 303 Squadron during the Battle of Britain had also flown in the Battle of France.

Force, and seemed doubtful of the Poles' competence and morale in light of their defeat in September. However, the RAF agreed to the formation of two active and two reserve bomber squadrons, and a number of Polish airmen began arriving in England for conversion training on British aircraft in late 1939 and early 1940.

Then France surrendered. The Battle of Britain began. The British situation quickly became desperate. Polish airmen were soon welcomed as much-needed reinforcements for the severely stretched RAF.[3]

The outstanding performance of 303 Squadron and the other Polish fighter pilots who flew in alliance with the RAF during the Battle of Britain, reinforced by the excellent records compiled by all the Polish Air Force units in the subsequent years of the war, changed British war-time perceptions: Polish airmen were soon held in the highest regard.

The Polish Air Force remained based in Britain throughout the balance of World War II.

Until the War's End

303 Squadron has become the iconic Polish air unit and its Battle of Britain successes are synonymous with the entire Polish air effort in World War II. But 303 Squadron was just one of many squadrons and the Battle of Britain just one of many battles that involved airmen with 'POLAND' shoulder patches.

Throughout the war, the Polish Air Force was by far the largest air force-in-exile of any of the German-occupied nations.

---

[3] Pursuant to agreement between the British government and the Polish government-in-exile, Polish airmen served during the Battle of Britain as members of the Polish Air Force allied with Great Britain, under operational control of the British in their capacity as Allied High Command.

Polish airmen served in fighter and bomber squadrons. They flew with all-Polish squadrons,[4] and individually within other Allied squadrons. They undertook defensive and offensive missions, as the nature of the war shifted. They fought in all the major campaigns: in Poland, France, Britain; at Dieppe and the Normandy landings; in the Battle of the Atlantic; in Germany, North Africa, Sicily, Italy. They undertook reconnaissance, army co-operation, anti-submarine, coastal patrol, balloon duty, and special duty (dropping supplies and parachutists over occupied Europe, including their homeland Poland). They served as part of the post-war occupation force in Germany.

Polish women joined the Women's Auxiliary Air Force ('WAAF'), and worked as drivers, fitters and armourers. And even in exile, the Polish Air Force maintained extensive training programmes for both pilots and ground crew, as well as its own Staff College.

Polish airmen served with distinction in combat operations from the very first day of World War II until the war's end in Europe—an end that proved more bitter than sweet for the gallant Polish men and women who had fought so long and so hard for freedom, when their American and British allies consigned Poland to the Soviet sphere of influence.

In a sense, World War II did not truly end for Poland until the fall of communism nearly fifty years later.

---

[4] A table of the Polish Air Force units formed while serving in alliance with the RAF during World War II is included as Appendix 9.

APPENDICES

APPENDIX 1

GLOSSARY OF
ENGLISH, POLISH, GERMAN AND FRENCH
TERMS AND ACRONYMS

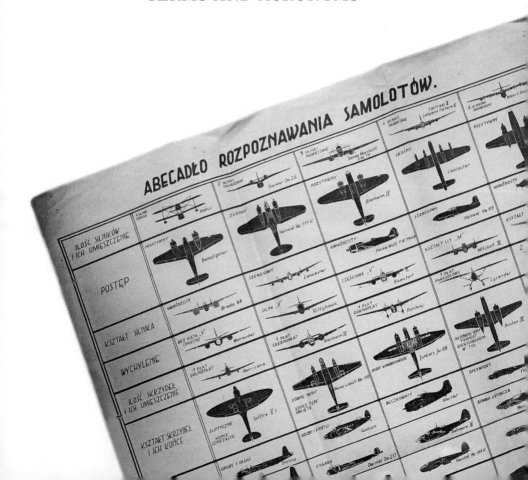

GLOSSARY OF

ENGLISH, POLISH, GERMAN AND FRENCH

TERMS AND ACRONYMS

ace	A pilot who downs five enemy aircraft
AK	Armia Krajowa (Home Army), the military arm of the Polish Underground State during World War II
AOC	Air Officer Commanding
ARP	Air Raid Precautions service, a British, mostly volunteer, organisation that helped protect civilians from the danger of air raids
Brygada Pościgowa	Pursuit Brigade, Polish Air Force (similar to an RAF wing), assigned to defend Warsaw during the German invasion of Poland in September 1939
CO	Commanding Officer
Croix de Guerre	Cross of War, a French military decoration
Cross of Valour	Krzyż Walecznych, a Polish military decoration
CzAF	Czechoslovak Air Force
DFC	Distinguished Flying Cross, a British military decoration
DFM	Distinguished Flying Medal, a British military decoration
DSO	Distinguished Service Order, a British military decoration

Dywizjon Myśliwski	Fighter Squadron, Polish Air Force
ECD	Escadrille de Chasse et de Défense (Fighter and Defence Flight), French Air Force
Eskadra Liniowa	Light Bomber Flight, Polish Air Force
Eskadra Myśliwska	Fighter Flight, Polish Air Force (similar to an RAF flight, of which there are usually two or three within a squadron); when Poland joined NATO in the late 1990s, this term was re-defined as a Fighter Squadron.
FTS	Flying Training School, RAF
GC	Groupe de Chasse (Fighter Group), French Air Force
HQ	Headquarters
Krzyż Walecznych	Cross of Valour, a Polish military decoration
Luftwaffe	The German air force
NCO	Non-Commissioned Officer
OBE	Officer of the Order of the British Empire, appointed for distinguished military or civil service
OC	Officer Commanding
OTU	Operational Training Unit, RAF
PAF	Polish Air Force
port	A nautical and aviation term designating the direction 'left'
POW	Prisoner of war
PRU	Photo Reconnaissance Unit, RAF
Pułk Lotniczy	Air Regiment, Polish Air Force (similar to both an RAF station and an RAF wing)

R and R	Rest and recreation
RAE	Royal Aircraft Establishment, a British research facility
RAF	Royal Air Force, Great Britain
RCAF	Royal Canadian Air Force
SFTS	Service Flying Training School
SPL	Szkoła Podchorążych Lotnictwa (Air Force Cadet Officers' School), the Polish Air Force College located at Dęblin, Poland, which has been known by various names since its formation in the 1920s
SPLdM	Szkoła Podoficerów Lotnictwa dla Małoletnich (Air Force NCO School for Minors), originally located at Bydgoszcz, in 1938 moved to Krosno, Poland; trained both air and ground crews
SPP	Szkoła Podchorążych Piechoty (Infantry Cadet Officers' School)
starboard	A nautical and aviation term designating the direction 'right'
USAAF	U.S. Army Air Forces (predecessor to the U.S. Air Force)
Virtuti Militari	Poland's highest military decoration

AIRCRAFT ABBREVIATIONS

GERMAN AIRCRAFT

Do 17	Dornier 17—bomber
Do 215	Dornier 215—bomber

CONTINUED: **GERMAN AIRCRAFT**

Fw 58	Focke-Wulf 58—multi-role aircraft, designed principally for advanced training of Luftwaffe personnel
Fw 190	Focke-Wulf 190—fighter
He 111	Heinkel 111—bomber
Hs 123	Henschel 123—dive-bomber and close-support attack aircraft
Hs 126	Henschel 126—reconnaissance and observation aircraft
Ju 87	Junkers 87—famous 'Stuka' dive bomber and ground-attack aircraft
Ju 88	Junkers 88—multi-role aircraft
Me 109	Messerschmitt 109—fighter
Me 110	Messerschmitt 110—fighter

FRENCH AIRCRAFT

M.B. 152	Bloch M.B. 152—fighter
M.S. 406	Morane-Saulnier M.S. 406—fighter

POLISH AIRCRAFT

MiG-29	Mikoyan MiG-29—Russian-built fighter
P. 11	PZL P. 11—fighter

AMERICAN AIRCRAFT

Mustang III	North American P-51 Mustang—fighter
P-40K-1	Curtiss P-40K-1—fighter

JAPANESE AIRCRAFT

Ki-44	Nakajima Ki-44—fighter

POLISH AIR FORCE RANKS AND THEIR ROYAL AIR FORCE EQUIVALENTS DURING WORLD WAR II

POLISH AIR FORCE RANKS AND

THEIR ROYAL AIR FORCE EQUIVALENTS

DURING WORLD WAR II

The agreements between the Polish Air Force and the RAF, under which the Polish Air Force served in alliance with the RAF during World War II, introduced a rather complicated system of ranks for Polish airmen. During this period, Polish airmen actually had three ranks: their Polish substantive rank; a British 'permanent war' rank which was meant to be equivalent to the Polish one, but often was not; and a British acting rank, which was a function of the appointment currently held. Hence a Pole could be a substantive Polish Captain, but an RAF Squadron Leader, or a substantive Polish Major, but an RAF Flight Lieutenant. A table of Polish Air Force and RAF rank equivalents is included below.

Polish Air Force regulations required its members to wear their British rank on their sleeves and their Polish rank on their lapels. Interestingly enough, many Polish airmen, especially in front-line units, frequently failed to do the latter— perhaps because for Polish Air Force operational personnel, the British ranks were more important as these defined their pay scales.

Neither the British Army nor the Royal Navy adopted these practices.

POLISH AIR FORCE RANKS
AND THEIR ROYAL AIR FORCE EQUIVALENTS
DURING WORLD WAR II

Royal Air Force	Polish Air Force[1]	Translation
Air Chief Marshal	*Generał Broni*	General
Air Marshal	*Generał Dywizji*	Lieutenant General
Air Vice-Marshal	*Generał Brygady*	Major General
Air Commodore[2]	–	–
Group Captain	*Pułkownik*	Colonel
Wing Commander	*Podpułkownik*	Lieutenant Colonel
Squadron Leader	*Major*	Major
Flight Lieutenant	*Kapitan*	Captain
Flying Officer	*Porucznik*	Lieutenant
Pilot Officer	*Podporucznik*	Second Lieutenant
Warrant Officer	*Chorąży*	Warrant Officer
Flight Sergeant	*Starszy Sierżant*	Senior Sergeant
Sergeant	*Sierżant*	Sergeant
Corporal	*Plutonowy*	Platoon Commander
Leading Aircraftman	*Kapral*	Corporal
Aircraftman 1st class	*Starszy Szeregowiec*	Senior Private
Aircraftman 2nd class	*Szeregowiec*	Private

[1] The words *'pilot,' 'nawigator,' 'obserwator'* or *'inżynier'* were added, when appropriate. Translator's note.

[2] The Poles did not have this rank. However, given the British practice of awarding the Poles acting or functional rank based on current appointments, a number of Polish officers wore the insignia of an Air Commodore, while holding a different Polish substantive rank. Translator's note.

303 SQUADRON PERSONNEL

IN THE BATTLE OF BRITAIN

APPENDIX 3

303 SQUADRON PERSONNEL

IN THE BATTLE OF BRITAIN

All the pilots of 303 Squadron during the Battle of Britain, both Polish and those of other nationalities, are listed below. This table also includes members of the squadron's ground crew mentioned by Arkady Fiedler in *303 Squadron*.

In writing *303 Squadron*, Fiedler focused on only a handful of the squadron's pilots. Those members of the squadron mentioned by Fiedler are indicated below in **bold** and brief biographies of those pilots are included as Appendix 4.

An internal memo from the British Air Ministry dated 14 October 1940, reporting on interrogations of captured German pilots during the Battle of Britain, ends with this warning:

> As a footnote, don't forget that it is absolutely forbidden to publish the names of Polish, Czech, Belgian, Dutch, Norwegian, or French airmen. This is in order to safeguard their relatives.

In order to protect the airmen of 303 Squadron, and their families who remained in occupied Poland, from German reprisals, Fiedler used pseudonyms. He included the following footnote in his original edition: 'All the names in this book are fictitious. The true names will be given in post-war editions.'

Following up on Fiedler's promise, this new English-language edition of *303 Squadron* (the first post-war edition of

233

Dywizjon 303 to be published in English), uses the true names of the airmen in 303 Squadron. The table below identifies each airman mentioned in Fiedler's book with the pseudonym given him in 1942.

This table also includes the RAF and Polish Air Force ranks of these airmen during the Battle of Britain. In cases where an airman was promoted during the Battle of Britain, both his initial rank and his rank following such promotion are indicated. Of course, as the war continued over the next five years, most of those airmen who survived would have received additional promotions. For more information about the ranks of members of the Polish Air Force who flew in alliance with the RAF during World War II, see Appendix 2 (Polish Air Force Ranks and their Royal Air Force Equivalents During World War II).

303 SQUADRON—POLISH PILOTS
IN THE BATTLE OF BRITAIN

RAF Rank	PAF Rank	True Name	Pseudonym in 1942 Edition
Sergeant	Sergeant	**Tadeusz Andruszków**	Sergeant Andrusz; Sergeant Andro
Sergeant	Sergeant	Marian Bełc	—
Sergeant	Sergeant	**Michał Brzezowski**	Sergeant Brzeza
Flying Officer	Lieutenant	**Arsen Cebrzyński**	Flying Officer Arsen
Pilot Officer	Second Lieutenant	**Jan Daszewski**	Joe
Pilot Officer	Second Lieutenant	**Mirosław Ferić**	Pilot Officer Ox; Flying Officer Ox
Sergeant	Sergeant	Paweł Gallus	—
Flying Officer	Lieutenant	Bogdan Grzeszczak	—
Flying Officer	Lieutenant	**Zdzisław Henneberg**	Pilot Officer Dzidek; Flying Officer Dzidek
Flying Officer	Lieutenant	Jerzy Jankiewicz	—
Flying Officer	Lieutenant	Wojciech Januszewicz	—
Sergeant	Sergeant	**Stanisław Karubin**	Sergeant Kar

Continued

APPENDIX 3

RAF Rank	PAF Rank	True Name	Pseudonym in 1942 Edition
Sergeant	Sergeant	Jan Kowalski	—
Squadron Leader	Major	**Zdzisław Krasnodębski**	Squadron Leader Krol
Flying Officer	Lieutenant	Wacław Łapkowski	—
Pilot Officer	Second Lieutenant	**Witold 'Tolo' Łokuciewski**	Pilot Officer Tolo
Pilot Officer	Second Lieutenant	Bogusław Mierzwa	—
Pilot Officer	Second Lieutenant	Włodzimierz Miksa	—
Flying Officer	Captain	Jerzy Orzechowski[1]	—
Sergeant	Sergeant	Jan Palak	—
Pilot Officer	Second Lieutenant	Jerzy Palusiński	—
Flying Officer; Acting Flight Lieutenant	Lieutenant	**Ludwik Paszkiewicz**	Pilot Officer Paszko; Flying Officer Paszko
Sergeant	Sergeant	Edward Paterek	—
Flying Officer	Lieutenant	**Marian Pisarek**	Flying Officer Pis
Pilot Officer	Second Lieutenant	Jerzy Radomski	—
Sergeant	Sergeant	Jan Rogowski	—
Flying Officer	Lieutenant	Tadeusz Sawicz	—
Sergeant	Sergeant	Antoni Siudak	—
Sergeant	Sergeant Cadet-Officer	Henryk Skowron	—
Sergeant	Corporal	Leon Świtoń	—
Sergeant	Sergeant	**Eugeniusz Szaposznikow**	Sergeant Szaposzka
Flying Officer; Acting Squadron Leader	Lieutenant	**Witold Urbanowicz**	Flight Officer Witur; Flight Lieutenant Witur; Squadron Leader Witur;
Sergeant	Sergeant	Mirosław Wojciechowski	—
Sergeant	Sergeant	**Stefan Wójtowicz**	Sergeant Wojt
Sergeant	Sergeant	**Kazimierz Wünsche**	Sergeant Zycz
Flying Officer	Lieutenant	Walerian Żak	—
Pilot Officer	Second Lieutenant	**Jan Zumbach**	Pilot Officer Jan Donald

[1] Orzechowski was posted briefly to No. 303 Squadron, but did not fly any missions with the squadron before being re-posted.

303 SQUADRON—OTHER PILOTS
IN THE BATTLE OF BRITAIN

RAF Rank	PAF Rank	Nationality	True Name	Pseudonym in 1942 Edition
Flight Lieutenant	—	British	**Athol Forbes**	Flight Lieutenant F.
Sergeant	Sergeant	Czech	**Josef František**	Sergeant Frantisek
Sergeant; Flight Sergeant	Sergeant	Slovak	Jozef Káňa	—
Squadron Leader	—	British	**Ronald Kellett**	Squadron Leader K.; Flight Lieutenant K.
Flight Lieutenant	—	Canadian	**John Kent**	Flight Lieutenant K.

303 SQUADRON—GROUND CREW MENTIONED
BY ARKADY FIEDLER

RAF Rank	PAF Rank	True Name	Pseudonym in 1942 Edition
Not known	Captain	**Jarosław Giejsztowt**	the officer in charge of operational control
Flying Officer	Lieutenant	**Wacław Wiórkiewicz**	Lieutenant Konkretny
Pilot Officer; Flying Officer	Second Lieutenant; Lieutenant	**Dr. Zygmunt Wodecki**	the doctor
Not known	Captain	**Witold Żyborski**	Flight Lieutenant Z.; squadron adjutant; papa

APPENDIX 4

PILOT BIOGRAPHIES

Tadeusz Andruszków

Born on 18 November 1920 at Lwów in south-east Poland (now Lviv, Ukraine). Andruszków joined Szkoła Podoficerów Lotnictwa dla Małoletnich ('SPLdM' –Air Force NCO School for Minors) at Bydgoszcz in 1936. The school moved to Krosno in 1938, and he graduated in 1939 as a fighter pilot.

He was posted to 162 Eskadra Myśliwska (162nd Fighter Flight) of the 6 Pułk Lotniczy (6th Air Regiment) at Lwów. His unit was deployed to the Łódź area west of Warsaw during the Nazi German invasion of Poland in September 1939, but he did not participate in the fighting in Poland due to a shortage of aircraft. On 6 September Andruszków was wounded when the unit's road party was attacked by German aircraft near the village of Brzeziny. He was subsequently evacuated to Romania and thence to France.

Following conversion training on French aircraft, he was posted to the independent fighter section of Lieutenant Jan

Falkowski (one of numerous such sections formed by Polish fighter pilots). After the fall of France he was evacuated to Britain, where he arrived on 23 June 1940. Finishing a short conversion training at No. 5 Operational Training Unit ('OTU') at Aston Down, Gloucestershire, Andruszków was posted on 21 August 1940 to No. 303 Squadron.

On 15 September 1940 at 15:00 hrs. he was downed in air combat over Dartford, Kent. He baled out safely and landed unhurt.

On 27 September 1940 Andruszków was shot down over Horsham, West Sussex, at 09:35 hrs. and died in Hurricane I no. V6665 RF-J. He is buried at Northwood Cemetery, Middlesex, grave no. H 208. Andruszków was posthumously awarded the Cross of Valour (Krzyż Walecznych).

Aerial victories officially credited to Tadeusz Andruszków:

Date		Victories	PAF Aircraft	Aircraft No.	Squadron No.
15 September 1940	1/2*	Do 215 - destroyed	Hurricane I	P3939 RF-H	303
26 September 1940	1	Do 215 - destroyed	Hurricane I	V6665 RF-J	

* Shared with Sergeant Mirosław Wojciechowski.

TOTAL: 1 destroyed, 1 shared destroyed.

Tadeusz Andruszków's older brother Marian, who graduated from SPLdM in 1938, served as a radio-operator/air gunner with No. 305 Bomber Squadron and was killed in a flying accident on 14 November 1943.

Michał Brzezowski

Born on 26 February 1920 near Pinsk, at Dawidgrodek. In 1936, Brzezowski joined SPLdM at Bydgoszcz and completed his studies at Krosno, graduating in 1939 as a fighter pilot.

Brzezowski was then posted to 151 Eskadra Myśliwska of 5 Pułk Lotniczy at Wilno in north-east Poland (now Vilnius in Lithuania) and took part in fighting during the September 1939 campaign. On 18 September he crossed the Romanian border by air, landing at Cernauti (now Chernovtsy in Ukraine). He reached France where, following conversion training on French aircraft, he was posted to the Polish fighter section under Lieutenant Arsen Cebrzyński, attached to the French Groupe de Chasse ('GC') II/6 'Cigogne' (II/6 'Stork' Fighter Squadron). On 5 June 1940 he was shot down in air combat.

Following the fall of France, Brzezowski was evacuated to Britain, arriving there on 7 July 1940. Following a short conversion training at No. 5 OTU at Aston Down, Gloucestershire, on 21 August 1940 he was posted to No. 303 Squadron.

On 15 September 1940 Brzezowski was shot down and killed over the Thames Estuary in Hurricane I no. P3577 RF-E. He was posthumously awarded the Cross of Valour.

Date	Victories		PAF Aircraft	Aircraft No.	Squadron No.
15 June 1940	1/3	Hs 126 - destroyed	M.B. 152	—	GC II/6
11 September 1940	2	He 111 - destroyed	Hurricane I	V6667 RF-K	303

TOTAL: 2 destroyed, 1 shared destroyed.

Cross of Valour

Arsen Cebrzyński

Born on 8 March 1912 at Batumi in Georgia (then part of the Russian Empire). His mother Helena, née Obaszydze Heczynaszwili, was Georgian and herself a proficient pilot.

In 1932 Cebrzyński joined Szkoła Podchorążych Piechoty ('SPP'–Infantry Cadet Officers' School), but in 1933 transferred to Szkoła Podchorążych Lotnictwa ('SPL'–Air Force Cadet Officers' School) at Dęblin. He graduated in 1934, was commissioned as Second Lieutenant Navigator, and was posted to 1 Pułk Lotniczy in Warsaw. The following year he completed a flying training course at Dęblin, and subsequently an advanced flying course at Szkoła Wyższego Pilotażu (Advanced Flying School) at Grudziądz. He then returned to 1 Pułk Lotniczy as a fighter pilot with 111 Eskadra Myśliwska. On 17 March 1938, Cebrzyński was seriously injured in an accident on landing. In 1939 he qualified for studies at the Polish Staff College, but was unable to attend due to the outbreak of war.

In September 1939 Cebrzyński served as tactical (intelligence) officer in III/1 Dywizjon Myśliwski (III/1 Fighter Squadron). On 17 September he was with this unit when it crossed the Romanian border. Subsequently he travelled via Yugoslavia and Italy, arriving in France on 12 October. During the Battle of France, Cebrzyński led a Polish section in GC II/6. After the fall of France he was evacuated to Britain, arriving on 7 July 1940. On 21 August Cebrzyński was posted to No. 303 Squadron.

On 11 September 1940 at about 16:30 hrs., he was shot down and killed in Hurricane I no. V6667 RF-K during air combat over Pembury, Royal Tunbridge Wells, Kent. Cebrzyński is buried at Northwood Cemetery, Middlesex, grave no. H 187. He was awarded the Cross of Valour and two bars.

Aerial victories officially credited to Arsen Cebrzyński:

Date	Victories		PAF Aircraft	Aircraft No.	Squadron No.
3 September 1939	1/3	Me 110 - destroyed	P. 11c	—	III/1 Dywizjon
5 June 1940	1 1/2	He 111 - destroyed	M.B. 152	—	GC II/6
15 June 1940	1/3	Hs 126 - destroyed	M.B. 152	—	

TOTAL: 1 destroyed, 3 shared destroyed.

Jan Daszewski

Born on 5 April 1916. In 1936 he joined the SPL. Daszewski graduated in 1938, was commissioned as a fighter pilot, and was posted to 1 Pułk Lotniczy in Warsaw. There he joined the 112 Eskadra Myśliwska with which he flew until September 1939.

On 18 September Daszewski crossed the Romanian border with his unit. He reached France and underwent conversion training on French aircraft. Initially assigned to the section of Lieutenant Wacław Łapkowski, he was eventually posted to the fighter section of Captain Tadeusz Opulski in defence of Romorantin. After the fall of France, Daszewski was evacuated to Britain. Following conversion training on British aircraft, he was posted to No. 303 Squadron on 2 August 1940 as one of its initial group of pilots.

On 7 September 1940 Daszewski was shot down by a German fighter over the Thames Estuary. Heavily wounded, he baled out and was taken to Waldershire Hospital, Selstead, Kent.

Daszewski returned to No. 303 Squadron in December 1940. In September 1941 he was posted briefly to No. 3 Ferry Pilots Pool for a rest from operational flying, but returned to No. 303 Squadron by the end of the month. On 22 November 1941 he was appointed to command No. 303 Squadron's 'B' Flight. Wounded on 13 December 1941 when his Spitfire was hit over France, Daszewski managed to get back to base and land safely.

On 4 April 1942 he was shot down, and this time killed, in Spitfire VB no. AD455 RF-V. His body was lost at sea. Daszewski was awarded the Silver Cross of the Virtuti Militari, and the Cross of Valour and three bars.

Aerial victories officially credited to Jan Daszewski:

Date		Victories	PAF Aircraft	Aircraft No.	Squadron No.
1 September 1939	1	Ju 87 - destroyed	P. 11	—	112 Eskadra
1 June 1940	1	He 111 - destroyed	M.S. 406	—	Romorantin
7 September 1940	1	Do 215 - destroyed	Hurricane I	P3890 RF-N	303
	1	Do 215 - probable destroyed			
20 April 1941	1	Me 109 - probable destroyed	Spitfire IIA	P8041 RF-E	

TOTAL: 3 destroyed, 2 probable destroyed.

Mirosław Feric

Born on 17 June 1915 at Travnik near Sarajevo (Bosnia-Herzegovina). In 1919 Feric and his family moved to Ostrów Wielkopolski, Poland. In 1935 he joined SPL. He was commissioned in 1938 as a fighter pilot and was posted to 111 Eskadra Myśliwska of 1 Pułk Lotniczy in Warsaw.

During the September 1939 campaign, Feric fought in the Brygada Pościgowa (Pursuit Brigade) covering Warsaw. In one sortie, he was obliged to bale out of his severely damaged aircraft. On 17 September Feric crossed the Romanian border with his unit. He reached France on 30 October 1939. After conversion training on French fighters, he was posted to the fighter section of Major Zdzisław Krasnodębski attached to the French GC I/55, and subsequently re-posted to the section of Captain Kazimierz Kuzian based at Nantes.

Evacuated to Britain after the fall of France, Feric was posted to No. 303 Squadron on 2 August 1940 as one of its initial group of pilots. During his service with No. 303 Squadron, he founded the '303 Squadron Chronicle,' an informal squadron diary to which all the squadron's pilots contributed. In November 1941 Ferić was appointed 'A' Flight commander in No. 303 Squadron, but instead had to be hospitalised due to serious illness. In February 1942 he re-joined No. 303 Squadron at his own request.

On 14 February 1942 at about 10:00 hrs. Ferić was killed in an accident at Northolt, West London, during a routine formation flight in Spitfire VB no. BL432 RF-K. He is buried at Northwood Cemetery, Middlesex, grave no. H 232.

Ferić was awarded the Silver Cross of the Virtuti Militari, the Cross of Valour and two bars, and the British Distinguished Flying Cross ('DFC'). A primary school and a street are named after Ferić in his home town of Ostrów Wielkopolski, Poland.

Aerial victories officially credited to Mirosław Ferić:

Date	Victories		PAF Aircraft	Aircraft No.	Squadron No.
3 September 1939	1/3	Me 110 - destroyed	P. 11c	—	111 Eskadra
8 September 1939	1	Hs 123 - destroyed	P. 11c	—	
31 August 1940	1	Me 109 - destroyed	Hurricane I	P3974 RF-J	303
2 September 1940	1	Me 109 - probable destroyed	Hurricane I	R4178 RF-G	
6 September 1940	1	Me 109 - destroyed	Hurricane I	P3700 RF-E	
15 September 1940	1	Me 109 - destroyed	Hurricane I	R2685 RF-G	
	1	Me 110 - destroyed			
27 September 1940	1	Me 109 - destroyed	Hurricane I	V6681 RF-B	
	1	He 111 - destroyed			
5 October 1940	1	Me 110 - destroyed	Hurricane I	V6681 RF-B	
22 June 1941	1	Me 109 - destroyed	Spitfire II	P8385 RF-A	
27 June 1941	1	Me 109 - damaged	Spitfire II	P8385 RF-A	

TOTAL: 9 destroyed, 1 shared destroyed, 1 probable destroyed, 1 damaged.

Athol Forbes

Born in 1912 in London, England. Forbes joined the RAF in November 1935 on a short service commission. He was trained at No. 10 Flying Training School ('FTS') in February 1936, and subsequently completed his training at the School of Army Co-operation at Old Sarum, Wiltshire, in August 1937, where he remained as a staff pilot.

On 8 July 1940 Forbes was posted to No. 6 OTU for a fighter conversion course, and then to No. 303 Squadron as a British flight commander.

On 6 September 1940 Forbes was slightly wounded during a crash landing at Northolt, West London, and the next day he force-landed again, this time in Essex, receiving another slight wound. On 11 September Forbes was wounded for a third time, landing his damaged Hurricane at Heston, Middlesex.

On 17 October 1940 he was posted to command No. 66 Squadron. Forbes remained at this post until October 1941, and afterwards he was posted to HQ No. 10 Group RAF. In July 1943 he was promoted to Wing Commander and posted to No. 165 Wing in No. 222 Group in India. In August 1944 he was posted to HQ No. 221 Wing in Burma. Forbes left the RAF in 1948 as a Group Captain.

Forbes was appointed an Officer of the Order of the British Empire ('OBE'), and awarded a DFC and bar, and the Polish Silver Cross of the Virtuti Militari. He died in 1981.

Aerial victories officially credited to Athol Forbes:

Date	Victories		PAF Aircraft	Aircraft No.	Squadron No.
5 September 1940	1	Ju 88 - destroyed	Hurricane I	R4217 RF-V	303
6 September 1940	1	Me 109 - destroyed	Hurricane I	R4179 RF-Q	
	1	Me 109 - probable destroyed			
7 September 1940	1	Do 215 - destroyed	Hurricane I	R4217 RF-V	
11 September 1940	2	Do 215 - destroyed	Hurricane I	V7465 RF-V	
26 September 1940	1	He 111 - destroyed	Hurricane I	V7465 RF-V	
27 September 1940	1	He 111 - destroyed	Hurricane I	L2099 RF-O	
25 June 1941	1/2	He 111 - destroyed	Spitfire II	—	66
20 August 1941	1/2	Me 109 - destroyed	Spitfire II	—	

TOTAL: 7 destroyed, 2 shared destroyed, 1 probable destroyed.

Josef František

Born on 7 October 1914 at Dolní Otaslavice near Prostějov (now in the Czech Republic). In 1934 František joined Škola pro odborný dorost letectva (Air Force School of Young Specialists) of the Czechoslovak Air Force ('CzAF') at Prostějov.

Upon graduation, in August 1936 František was posted to the 2nd Air Regiment CzAF at Olomouc. In early 1938 he completed the fighter pilot's course at the 4th Air Regiment CzAF based at the Prague-Kbely airfield, and in May 1938 he was posted to the 40th Fighter Flight of that regiment. František was serving with that flight on 15 March 1939 when Nazi Germany occupied the entire Czech territory.

Following the German occupation, the Czechoslovak armed forces were dissolved; on 1 April 1939 František was released from service. Like many of his colleagues, František chose to leave his German-occupied homeland and go to Poland. With a number of other Czech airmen he took part in the

September 1939 campaign in the I Pluton (1st Platoon) of the Observer's Training Flight at the SPL.

In late September 1939 František crossed the Romanian border with this unit and made his way to France, travelling under a false Polish identity. In France he chose to stay in the Polish Air Force, even though Free CzAF units were formed in that country. František was posted with a group of Polish airmen to the air base at Clermont-Ferrand.

Aerial victories officially credited to Josef František:[*]

Date		Victories	PAF Aircraft	Aircraft No.	Squadron No.
2 September 1940	1	Me 109 - destroyed	Hurricane I	P3975 RF-U	
3 September 1940	1	'He 113'[**] - destroyed	Hurricane I	P3975 RF-U	
5 September 1940	1	Ju 88 - destroyed	Hurricane I	R4175 RF-R	
	1	Me 109 - destroyed			
6 September 1940	1	Me 109 - destroyed	Hurricane I	R4175 RF-R	
9 September 1940	1	Me 109 - destroyed	Hurricane I	P3975 RF-U	
	1	He 111 - destroyed			
11 September 1940	2	Me 109 - destroyed	Hurricane I	V7289 RF-S	303
	1	He 111 - destroyed			
15 September 1940	1	Me 110 - destroyed	Hurricane I	P3089 RF-S	
18 September 1940	1	Me 109 - destroyed	Hurricane I	V7465 RF-V	
26 September 1940	2	He 111 - destroyed	Hurricane I	R4175 RF-R	
27 September 1940	1	He 111 - destroyed	Hurricane I	R4175 RF-R	
	1	Me 110 - destroyed			
30 September 1940	1	Me 109 - destroyed	Hurricane I	L2099 RF-O	
	1	Me 109 - probable destroyed			

TOTAL: 17 destroyed, 1 probable destroyed.

[*] Some publications claim that he shot down ten or eleven German aircraft during the Battle of France, but this was probably due to confusion with another Czech ace, František Peřina, serv. no. 83231.

[**] Claimed by František and credited by RAF authorities as 'He 113,' but no such Heinkel type was actually in use during the Battle of Britain. The actual aircraft destroyed has not been positively identified.

Following the fall of France, František was evacuated to Britain. He was posted to No. 303 Squadron on 2 August 1940 as one of its initial group of pilots. Despite an unimpressive start (on 8 August he damaged a Hurricane when he forgot to extend the undercarriage for landing), he soon became a leading ace of the squadron and of the entire RAF Fighter Command.

On 9 September he was shot down and made a forced landing near Brighton, West Sussex. František was killed in a flying accident on 8 October 1940 at about 09:00 hrs. at Cuddington Way, Ewell, Surrey. He is buried at Northwood Cemetery, Middlesex, grave no. H 246.

František was awarded the Polish Silver Cross of the Virtuti Militari, the Polish Cross of Valour and two bars, the Czechoslovak War Cross, and the British Distinguished Flying Medal ('DFM') and bar. He was posthumously commissioned to an officer's rank.

A biography of František by Jiří Rajlich was published in English in 2010 under the title *Hurricane Ace Josef František —The True Story*.

Czechoslovak War Cross

Zdzisław Henneberg

Born on 11 May 1911 in Warsaw. Henneberg joined the SPL in 1932. He was commissioned as a navigator in 1934 and posted to 1 Pułk Lotniczy in Warsaw. The following year he completed a flying course and subsequently an advanced flying course that qualified him as a fighter pilot. As a pilot he flew in 111 Eskadra Myśliwska.

In 1937 Henneberg became an instructor at the SPL. At the same time he was a well-known sports-flyer in the Warsaw Flying Club, and in 1937 he represented Poland at the gliding championships at Rhön in Germany.

In September 1939 Henneberg fought in the so-called Dęblin Group, an ad hoc unit of flying instructors. He escaped via Romania to France. During the Battle of France he led the 'Chimney Flight,' officially known as Escadrille de Chasse et de Défense ('ECD'–Fighter and Defence Flight), in defence of the Bloch assembly plant at Châteauroux.

Following the French collapse, on 18 June 1940 Henneberg

led his unit (three fighters and a light transport aircraft) to RAF Tangmere in West Sussex, the only Polish unit to fly their aircraft from France to Britain. In Britain, after a short conversion training he was posted on 2 August 1940 to No. 303 Squadron as one of its initial group of pilots.

In early September 1940, Henneberg was appointed the Polish commander of the 'A' Flight in No. 303 Squadron. On 22 October 1940 he became acting commander of No. 303 Squadron, holding this post until 6 November 1940, after which he resumed his 'A' Flight commander duties. On 22 February 1941 he was again appointed to command No. 303 Squadron and held this post until his death several weeks later.

Aerial victories officially credited to Zdzisław Henneberg:

Date		Victories	PAF Aircraft	Aircraft No.	Squadron No.
5 June 1940	1/2	He 111 - destroyed	M.B. 152	—	ECD He*
31 August 1940	1	Me 109 - destroyed	Hurricane I	V7290 RF-H	303
2 September 1940	1	Me 109 - damaged	Hurricane I	V7246 RF-D	
7 September 1940	1	Me 109 - destroyed	Hurricane I	V6605 YO-N**	
	1	Me 109 - probable destroyed			
11 September 1940	1	He 111 - destroyed	Hurricane I	P3939 RF-H	
	1	Me 109 - destroyed			
15 September 1940	1	Me 109 - destroyed	Hurricane I	P3120 RF-A	
	1	Do 215 - destroyed			
27 September 1940	1	Me 109 - destroyed	Hurricane I	V7246 RF-D	
5 October 1940	1	Me 110 - destroyed	Hurricane I	V6684 RF-F	

* The Polish flights attached to French ECD units were named after the first letters of their OC's last name, thus 'ECD He' for the flight commanded by Henneberg.

** The Hurricane was borrowed from No. 1 Squadron RCAF, also based at Northolt, West London.

TOTAL: 8 destroyed, 1 shared destroyed, 1 probable destroyed, 1 damaged.

On 12 April 1941, during a combat mission to France, Henneberg's Spitfire II P8029 RF-P was damaged by German ground fire. He was forced to ditch in the English Channel off Dungeness, Kent, and was never found. Henneberg was awarded the Silver Cross of the Virtuti Militari, the Cross of Valour and bar, the British DFC, and the French Croix de Guerre.

Croix de Guerre

Stanisław Karubin

Born on 29 October 1915 in Warsaw. He completed his flying training at Szkoła Podoficerów Pilotów (NCO Pilots School) at Bydgoszcz. After his flying training he was posted in 1937 to 111 Eskadra Myśliwska in Warsaw, remaining with that unit during the September 1939 campaign.

Karubin escaped to France via Romania, and was posted to a Polish section under Major Krasnodębski attached to GC I/55. After France collapsed, he was evacuated to Britain. Following a brief conversion course, Karubin was posted to No. 303 Squadron on 2 August 1940 as one of its initial group of pilots.

On 6 September 1940 Karubin was shot down and wounded by return fire from German bombers. After three weeks in hospital, he returned to No. 303 Squadron. On 7 March 1941 Karubin was posted as an instructor to No. 57 OTU, and a month later to No. 55 OTU.

Karubin was killed on 12 August 1941 during a training

flight when his Hurricane I no. V7742 collided with high terrain at Horn Cragg, Cumberland. He is buried at Castletown Cemetery, Sunderland. Karubin was awarded the Silver Cross of the Virtuti Militari, the Cross of Valour and bar, and the British DFM.

Aerial victories officially credited to Stanisław Karubin:

Date		Victories	PAF Aircraft	Aircraft No.	Squadron No.
3 September 1939	1	Me 110 - destroyed	P. 11c	—	111 Eskadra
31 August 1940	1	Me 109 - destroyed	Hurricane I	R2688 RF-F	
5 September 1940	2	Me 109 - destroyed	Hurricane I	P3975 RF-U	
6 September 1940	1	He 111 - destroyed	Hurricane I	V7290 RF-H	303
30 September 1940	1	Me 109 - destroyed	Hurricane I	V7504 RF-G	
5 October 1940	1	Me 109 - destroyed	Hurricane I	P3901 RF-E	

TOTAL: 7 destroyed.

Distinguished Flying Medal

Ronald Kellett

Born on 13 September 1909 at Eldon, Durham, the son of a colliery owner. Kellett became a stockbroker, and in 1931 was an unsuccessful National Conservative candidate in the Parliamentary elections.

In 1933 Kellett joined No. 600 Squadron (Royal Auxiliary Air Force) for a five-year service. In the international tension of 1938–1939 he did not go onto the reserve, but was posted to No. 616 Squadron in early 1939. In May 1940 he was appointed a flight commander in No. 249 Squadron, and in June 1940 took command of that squadron.

In July 1940 Kellett became the British commander of No. 303 Squadron. On 6 September he was slightly wounded in air combat, but soon resumed flying. In December 1940 he was posted to command No. 96 Squadron, and in March 1941 he was promoted to lead the North Weald Wing in Essex. In mid-July 1941 he moved to a staff job at the Air Ministry.

At the end of 1942 Kellett attended the Senior Course at the

Army Staff College. In June 1943 he went to Turkey as a Staff College Instructor and stayed there for two years. He then returned to the U.K. and left the regular RAF service, but rejoined the Royal Auxiliary Air Force and commanded No. 615 Squadron from 1946 to 1948. He thereafter resumed his stock-broking activity, living in Kent.

Kellett was awarded the DFC, the Distinguished Service Order ('DSO'), and the Polish Silver Cross of the Virtuti Militari. He died on 1 November 1998.

Aerial victories officially credited to Ronald Kellett:

Date	Victories		PAF Aircraft	Aircraft No.	Squadron No.
31 August 1940	1	Me 109 - destroyed	Hurricane I	R4178 RF-G	
5 September 1940	1	Me 109 - destroyed	Hurricane I	V7284 RF-A	
	1	Me 109 - probable destroyed			
6 September 1940	1	Do 215 - destroyed	Hurricane I	V7284 RF-A	303
15 September 1940	1	Me 110 - destroyed	Hurricane I	V7465 RF-V	
	1	Do 215 - probable destroyed			
26 September 1940	1	Me 109 - destroyed	Hurricane I	V6681 RF-B	
5 October 1940	1	Me 109 - damaged	Hurricane I	V7504 RF-G	

TOTAL: 5 destroyed, 2 probable destroyed, 1 damaged.

John Kent

Born on 23 June 1914 in Winnipeg, Manitoba, Canada. Kent obtained his first pilot's licence in November 1930, and in June 1933, aged nineteen, he became the youngest professional pilot in Canada.

Kent joined the RAF in January 1935 on short service commission, and commenced training at No. 5 FTS in March. In February 1936 he joined No. 19 Squadron at Duxford, Cambridgeshire, flying Gloster Gauntlet open cockpit biplane fighters. In October 1937 Kent was posted to the Royal Aircraft Establishment ('RAE') at Farnborough in Kent as a test pilot. His duties there included crashing aircraft against barrage balloon cables! In January 1939 he was awarded the Air Force Cross for his achievements as a test pilot.

In May 1940 he joined the Photo Reconnaissance Unit ('PRU') at Heston, Middlesex, and was posted to No. 212 Squadron which was based in France as a detachment of the

PRU. There he flew reconnaissance missions in unarmed variants of the Spitfire. In July 1940 he underwent conversion training on Hurricanes at No. 7 OTU.

In July 1940, Kent was posted as the British commander of the 'A' Flight in No. 303 Squadron. On 6 September he was forced to land due to an engine fire in his Hurricane (a machine borrowed from a Canadian squadron).

In October 1940 Kent was appointed to command No. 92 Squadron on Spitfires. In March 1941 he was posted for a period of rest, becoming the Chief Instructor at No. 53 OTU. On 3 June 1941 he was appointed to lead the Polish Wing at Northolt, West London, but two months later, on 2 August 1941, he was re-posted to command Kenley Wing in the London Borough of Croydon. Wing leaders at the time were free to choose code letters on their aircraft; notably, both at Northolt and then at Kenley, Kent's aeroplane displayed the 'RF' code of No. 303 Squadron.

In October 1941 Kent returned to the post of No. 53 OTU Chief Instructor. In late 1941 he lectured in the United States and Canada. Upon his return to Britain in June 1942, Kent took command of RAF Station Church Fenton in North Yorkshire. From October he held a staff post in London, but in December 1942 he was posted to command No. 17 Sector RAF at Benghazi, Libya, in North Africa. He then held a number of command posts in the Mediterranean, before returning to Britain in mid-1944, where he commanded No. 3 (Pilots) Advanced Flying Unit. In 1945 he completed a course at the RAF Staff College and then he served at the HQ British Air Forces of Occupation.

In 1947 Kent was appointed the chief test pilot at RAE Farnborough. In the early 1950s he was posted on an exchange tour at the USAAF base Wright-Patterson in Ohio. Back in

Britain, in August 1952 he was appointed to command RAF Station Odiham, Berkshire, and then RAF Tangmere, West Sussex.

Kent retired from the RAF on 1 December 1956 at the rank of Group Captain. Thereafter he was active in the aviation business. His memoir, entitled *One of the Few*, was first published in 1971. Kent died on 7 October 1985 in England. He was awarded the DFC and bar, and the Polish Silver Cross of the Virtuti Militari.

Aerial victories officially credited to John Kent:

Date		Victories	PAF Aircraft	Aircraft No.	Squadron No.
9 September 1940	1	Me 110 - destroyed	Hurricane I	V6665 RF-J	303
	1	Ju 88 - probable destroyed			
23 September 1940	1	Me 109 - destroyed	Hurricane I	V6681 RF-B	
	1	Fw 58 - damaged			
27 September 1940	1	Ju 88 - destroyed	Hurricane I	V6684 RF-F	
1 October 1940	1	Me 109 - destroyed	Hurricane I	V6681 RF-B	
	1	Me 109 - probable destroyed			
1 November 1940	1	Me 109 - destroyed	Spitfire I	X4606	92
2 November 1940	2	Me 109 - destroyed	Spitfire I	X4606	
	1	Me 109 - probable destroyed			
21 June 1941	1	Me 109 - destroyed	Spitfire II	P8189 RF-J	Northolt Wing
3 July 1941	1	Me 109 - destroyed	Spitfire II	P8518 RF-J	
20 July 1941	1	Me 109 - destroyed	Spitfire II	P8518 RF-J	
7 August 1941	1	Me 109 - destroyed	Spitfire II	P8518 RF-J	Kenley Wing
16 August	1	Me 109 - destroyed	Spitfire V	AB790	
25 January 1943	1	Ju 88 - damaged	Hurricane	DG-H	17 Sector

TOTAL : 12 destroyed, 3 probable destroyed, 2 damaged.

Zdzisław Krasnodębski

Born on 10 July 1904 at Wola Osowińska near Łuków in the Lublin area. In 1920 Krasnodębski joined the Polish Army as a volunteer during the Polish–Bolshevik War of 1919–1920. In 1925 he joined the Oficerska Szkoła Lotnictwa (Air Force Officers' School), which in 1927 was renamed the SPL. He was commissioned in 1928 as a Second Lieutenant Navigator.

In 1929 Krasnodębski completed his flying training. He flew in fighter units of 1 Pułk Lotniczy in Warsaw. On 13 November 1935 he was appointed officer commanding 111 Eskadra Myśliwska. In September 1939 he commanded III/1 Dywizjon Myśliwski within the Brygada Pościgowa. Krasnodębski was shot down in air combat on 3 September 1939, baling out with slight burns. On 17 September he crossed the Romanian border with his unit, and reached France in October 1939.

Following conversion training on French fighter aircraft,

Krasnodębski led the Polish section of GC I/55 at Étampes. After the fall of France, he arrived in Britain on 22 June 1940. In July he was appointed the first Polish commander of the new all-Polish fighter unit that soon became No. 303 Squadron.

On 6 September 1940 Krasnodębski was shot down in air combat. He baled out from his Hurricane I no. P3974 RF-J with serious burns. In the Queen Victoria Hospital at East Grinstead in West Sussex, the famous surgeon Archie McIndoe performed plastic surgery on him (thus Krasnodębski joined the famed 'Guinea Pig Club').

In mid-1941 Krasnodębski was posted to the Polish Military Mission in Canada, and then lectured in the United States. On 23 March 1943 he returned to Britain. On 1 April 1943 he was appointed Polish commander at RAF Station Heston, Middlesex. On 4 October 1943 he took command of the newly formed No. 131 (Polish) Airfield 2nd Tactical Air Force, which he led until 17 February 1944. On 25 February 1944 he was posted to the General Staff.

In 1945 Krasnodębski completed a course at the Wyższa Szkoła Lotnicza (Polish Air Force Staff College). On 15 October 1945 he was appointed Polish commander at RAF Station Newton, home of No. 16 (Polish) Service Flying Training School ('SFTS'). He remained at this post until released from the Polish Air Force. In 1948 he emigrated to South Africa, then in 1951 to Canada.

Krasnodębski was awarded the Silver Cross of the Virtuti Militari, and the Cross of Valour. He died on 3 August 1980 in Toronto.

Aerial victories officially credited to Zdzisław Krasnodębski:

Date	Victories		PAF Aircraft	Aircraft No.	Squadron No.
3 September 1939	1/3	Me 110 - destroyed	P. 11c	—	III/1 Dywizjon

TOTAL: 1 shared destroyed.

Witold Łokuciewski

Born on 1 February 1917 in Russia, at Novocherkask-on-Don. In 1918 Łokuciewski moved to Poland with his parents, and the family settled in Wilno. In 1935 he joined Szkoła Podchorążych Rezerwy Kawalerii (Cavalry Reserve Cadet Officers' School), and the following year the SPL.

Łokuciewski was commissioned in 1938 as a fighter pilot and obtained his first posting to 1 Pułk Lotniczy in Warsaw. In September 1939 he fought with 112 Eskadra Myśliwska. After the Soviet invasion of Poland on 17 September 1939, Łokuciewski crossed into Romania with his unit and subsequently made his way to France via Yugoslavia and Italy. He flew in combat in the fighter section of Captain Opulski, in defence of industrial facilities at Romorantin.

After the fall of France he was evacuated to Britain. On 2 August 1940 Łokuciewski was posted to No. 303 Squadron as one of its initial group of pilots. On 15 September 1940 he was wounded during air combat. On 3 April 1941 he was slightly injured in an accident.

On 21 November 1941 Łokuciewski was appointed 'B' Flight commander in No. 303 Squadron. On 13 March 1942 he was shot down in air combat over France and became a prisoner of war. From July 1942 until January 1945 he was at the Stalag Luft III POW camp. In 1943 he escaped, but was recaptured at Liegnitz (now Legnica in Poland).

Aerial victories officially credited to Witold Łokuciewski:

Date		Victories	PAF Aircraft	Aircraft No.	Squadron No.
1 September 1939	1/2	Ju 87 - probable destroyed	P. 11	—	112 Eskadra
10 June 1940	1	He 111 - destroyed	M.S. 406	—	Romorantin
7 September 1940	1	Do 215 - destroyed	Hurricane I	P3975 RF-U	303
	1	Do 215 - probable destroyed	Hurricane I		
11 September 1940	1	Do 215 - destroyed	Hurricane I	L2099 RF-O	
	1	Me 109 - destroyed			
15 September 1940	1	Me 109 - destroyed	Hurricane I	P2903 RF-Z	
20 April 1941	1	Me 109 - destroyed	Spitfire II	P7546 RF-T	
18 June 1941	1	Me 109 - destroyed	Spitfire II	P8333 RF-S	
22 June 1941	1	Me 109 - destroyed	Spitfire II	P8333 RF-S	
	1	Me 109 - probable destroyed			
11 July 1941	1	Me 109 - probable destroyed	Spitfire II	P8333 RF-S	

TOTAL: 8 destroyed, 3 probable destroyed, 1 shared probable destroyed.

After liberation in April 1945, Łokuciewski returned from Germany to Britain. In September 1945 he was posted to HQ of the 3rd Polish Wing at Andrews Field, Essex. On 29 November 1945 he was re-posted back to No. 303 Squadron and on

1 February 1946 he took command of that squadron as its last commander.

Łokuciewski returned to Poland in June 1947. In November 1956 he was recruited into the Polish Air Force and underwent conversion training on MiG-15 jet fighters. From 1969 to 1972 he was the military, naval and air attaché at the Polish Embassy in London, but was ostracised by his former colleagues who had chosen to remain in the U.K. rather than return to the post-war communist-controlled Poland.

He was awarded the Silver Cross of the Virtuti Militari, the Cross of Valour and bar, and the British DFC. Łokuciewski died on 17 April 1990 in Warsaw. His biography by Bożena Gostkowska was published in 2007 under the title *TOLO–Muszkieter z Dywizjonu 303* (*TOLO–Musketeer from 303 Squadron*).

Ludwik Paszkiewicz

Born on 21 October 1907 at Wola Gałęzowska in the Lublin region. Paszkiewicz studied at the Politechnika Lwówska (Lwów Technical University). In 1932 he completed a course at Szkoła Podchorążych Rezerwy Lotnictwa (Air Force Reserve Cadet Officer's School), after which he joined the SPL in 1932.

Paszkiewicz was commissioned in 1934 and posted to 12 Eskadra Liniowa (12th Light Bomber Flight) of 1 Pułk Lotniczy in Warsaw. After an advanced flying course (April to July 1936) he was posted to 112 Eskadra Myśliwska in August 1936. On 1 August 1938 he was appointed tactics (intelligence) officer of III/1 Dywizjon Myśliwski of 1 Pułk Lotniczy.

In August 1939 he left for France with a Polish military mission for a Morane-Saulnier M.S. 406 fighter-handling course. Upon completion of the course he went to Britain, planning to fly a Fairey Battle bomber to Poland, but this plan was abandoned due to the outbreak of war and defeat of Poland in

September. During the Battle of France in 1940 he led a Polish section attached to GC II/8. Evacuated to Britain, Paszkiewicz was posted on 2 August 1940 to No. 303 Squadron as one of its original group of pilots, becoming the Polish commander of 'B' Flight.

On 30 August 1940 Paszkiewicz shot down a Messerschmitt 110 (claimed as a Do 215) during a training sortie, obtaining the first kill for No. 303 Squadron even before that squadron was officially operational.

On 27 September 1940, at about 09:20 hrs. Paszkiewicz was shot down and killed over Borough Green, Kent, in Hurricane I no. L1696 RF-T. He is buried at Northwood Cemetery, Middlesex, grave no. H 224. Paszkiewicz was awarded the Silver Cross of the Virtuti Militari.

Aerial victories officially credited to Ludwik Paszkiewicz:

Date		Victories	PAF Aircraft	Aircraft No.	Squadron No.
30 August 1940	1	'Do 215'* - destroyed	Hurricane I	R4217 RF-V	
7 September 1940	2	Do 215 - destroyed	Hurricane I	V7235 RF-M	
11 September 1940	1	Me 110 - destroyed	Hurricane I	V7235 RF-M	303
15 September 1940	1	Me 109 - destroyed	Hurricane I	V7235 RF-M	
26 September 1940	1	He 111 - destroyed	Hurricane I	V7235 RF-M	

* Claimed as 'Do 215' but was in fact Messerschmitt Bf 110C W.Nr.3615 M8+MM of 4./ZG76, which crashed at Barley Beans Farm, Kimpton, Hertfordshire.

TOTAL: 6 destroyed.

Marian Pisarek

Born on 3 January 1912 at Łosie near Radzymin, east of Warsaw. In 1932, Pisarek joined the SPP. Commissioned in 1934, he was posted to the 4 Pułk Strzelców Podhalańskich (4th Regiment of Highland Fusiliers).

Pisarek volunteered to join the Polish Air Force in 1935 and completed a flying course. He was posted to 61 Eskadra Liniowa of 6 Pułk Lotniczy at Lwów. After completing an advanced flying course in 1936, he received posting to 142 Eskadra Myśliwska of 4 Pułk Lotniczy at Toruń. In 1937 he transferred to 141 Eskadra Myśliwska with which he took part in fighting in the September 1939 campaign.

From 3 September 1939 Pisarek commanded 141 Eskadra. On 18 September he crossed the Romanian border with his unit, and found his way to France via Yugoslavia and Italy. In 1940 he was posted to the fighter section of Captain Tadeusz Rolski. During the evacuation after the fall of France, Pisarek joined the group of Major Krasnodębski. He arrived in Britain on 23 June 1940 and was posted to No. 303 Squadron on 21 August 1940.

On 7 September 1940 Pisarek was shot down and baled out safely, but his aeroplane crashed behind the house at 40 Roding Road, Loughton, Essex, killing three civilians. From 29 September until 11 November 1940 he was the Polish commander of 'B' Flight in No. 303 Squadron.

Aerial victories officially credited to Marian Pisarek:

Date		Victories	PAF Aircraft	Aircraft No.	Squadron No.
1 September 1939	1/2	Hs 126 - destroyed	P. 11c	—	141 Eskadra
2 September 1939	1	Hs 126 - destroyed	P. 11c	—	
	1	Do 17 - destroyed			
4 September 1939	1	Ju 87 - damaged	P. 11c	—	
7 September 1940	1	Me 109 - destroyed	Hurricane I	R4173 RF-T	303
15 September 1940	1	Me 109 - destroyed	Hurricane I	V7465 RF-V	
5 October 1940	1	Me 110 - destroyed	Hurricane I	V7503 RF-U	
	1	Me 110 - damaged			
7 October 1940	1	Me 109 - destroyed	Hurricane I	V7503 RF-U	
2 July 1941	1	Me 109 - destroyed	Spitfire IIB	P7446 ZF-A	308
17 July 1941	1/2	Me 109 - destroyed	Spitfire IIB	P8676 ZF-H	
22 July 1941	1	Me 109 - probable destroyed	Spitfire IIB	P8341 ZF-A	
14 August 1941	1	Me 109 - destroyed	Spitfire IIB	P8318	
20 September 1941	1	Me 109 - destroyed	Spitfire VB	W3702	
21 September 1941	1	Me 109 - destroyed	Spitfire VB	AB825	
13 October 1941	1	Me 109 - destroyed	Spitfire VB	W3798	

TOTAL: 11 destroyed, 2 shared destroyed, 1 probable destroyed, 2 damaged.

Pisarek transferred to No. 315 Squadron, then being formed at Acklington, Northumberland, on 21 January 1941. Two months later, on 30 March 1941, he was posted to No. 308 Squadron as 'A' Flight commander. From 23 June until

10 December 1941, Pisarek commanded No. 308 Squadron. On 24 July 1941 his Spitfire was seriously damaged over France when his wingman collided with him, but he managed to bring it back to base.

In December 1941 Pisarek was posted to HQ No. 11 Fighter Group as the Polish Liaison Officer. On 17 April 1942 he assumed command of the 1st Polish Fighter Wing at Northolt, West London. He was shot down and killed on 29 April 1942 when leading his wing over France.

Pisarek was awarded the Golden Cross of the Virtuti Militari (posthumously), the Silver Cross of the Virtuti Militari, the Cross of Valour and three bars, and the British DFC. A street in Warsaw was named after him in 1979, as was a primary school at Radzymin in 1991. His biography by Krzysztof Kubala was published in Polish in 2005 under the title *Start w nieskończoność* (*Take-off Into Eternity*).

Silver Cross of the Virtuti Militari

Eugeniusz Szaposznikow

Eugeniusz Szaposznikow was born on 17 July 1917 in Warsaw. He completed a course of flying training in 111 Eskadra Myśliwska of 1 Pułk Lotniczy in Warsaw as a corporal.

He fought in the September 1939 campaign in 111 Eskadra Myśliwska within Brygada Pościgowa. Szaposznikow escaped to France via Romania, and during the Battle of France he flew in the Polish section led by Lieutenant Arsen Cebrzyński in GC II/6.

After the fall of France Szaposznikow evacuated to Britain. On 2 August 1940, after a short conversion training, he was posted to No. 303 Squadron as one of its initial group of pilots.

On 14 May 1941 Szaposznikow was posted to No. 8 FTS at Montrose in Scotland as a flying instructor. In November 1941 he was commissioned as an officer. On 4 January 1942 he was posted to the Flying Instructor's School at Church Lawford, Warwickshire. After completion of the course he went to No. 16 (Polish) SFTS at Newton in Nottinghamshire.

APPENDIX 4

Szaposznikow resumed combat flying on 14 December
1943, joining No. 316 Squadron, but a week later he was
transferred back to No. 303 Squadron. On 8 April 1944 he
suffered a serious accident when his wingman collided with
him on the runway, but he escaped unhurt. On 6 July 1944
he was appointed 'A' Flight commander in No. 303 Squadron. On
14 November 1944 Szaposznikow returned to instructor duties
at No. 16 (Polish) SFTS.

After disbandment of the Polish Air Force in 1946,
Szaposznikow settled in Britain and subsequently changed his
name to Sharman. He was awarded the Silver Cross of the
Virtuti Militari, the Cross of Valour and three bars, and the
British DFM. Szaposznikow died in Nottingham on 8 July 1991.

Aerial victories officially credited to Eugeniusz Szaposznikow:

Date		Victories	PAF Aircraft	Aircraft No.	Squadron No.
15 June 1940	1/3	Hs 126 - destroyed	M.B. 152	—	GC II/6
31 August 1940	1	Me 109 - destroyed	Hurricane I	V7242 RF-B	
7 September 1940	1	Do 215 - destroyed	Hurricane I	V7244 RF-C	
	1	Me 109 - destroyed			
11 September 1940	2	Me 110 - destroyed	Hurricane I	V7244 RF-C	303
23 September 1940	1	Me 109 - destroyed	Hurricane I	V7244 RF-C	
27 September 1940	1	Me 109 - destroyed	Hurricane I	V7244 RF-C	
7 October 1940	1	Me 109 - destroyed	Hurricane I	V7244 RF-C	
	1	Me 109 - damaged			

TOTAL: 8 destroyed, 1 shared destroyed, 1 damaged.

Witold Urbanowicz

Born on 30 March 1908 at Olszanka near Augustów. In 1930 Urbanowicz joined the SPL. He was commissioned on 15 August 1932 as a Second Lieutenant Navigator, and posted to the 213 Nocna Eskadra Bombowa (213rd Night Bomber Flight) of 1 Pułk Lotniczy in Warsaw.

In 1933 Urbanowicz completed a flying training course and an advanced flying course. As a pilot he flew in 113 Eskadra Myśliwska and then 111 Eskadra Myśliwska. In August 1936 he shot down a Soviet reconnaissance aircraft that had violated Polish air space. In late 1936 he returned to Dęblin as an instructor and head of a class.

In the September 1939 campaign, Urbanowicz fought within the so-called Dęblin Group. He then nursed his entire group of cadet-officers through Romania and by sea to Marseilles, and he subsequently volunteered for training in Britain, arriving on 27 January 1940 with one of the first group of Polish airmen.

After conversion training on British equipment at No. 6 OTU, Urbanowicz was posted on 4 August 1940 to No. 145 Squadron. In early August, he flew some aircraft of No. 601 Squadron, and in mid-August he was briefly attached to No. 253 Squadron. On 21 August 1940 he was posted to No. 303 Squadron as 'A' Flight commander. On 7 September 1940, after Squadron Leader Zdzisław Krasnodębski was wounded in combat, Urbanowicz assumed command of the squadron. Urbanowicz was the top-scoring Polish pilot in the Battle of Britain, credited with 15 aerial victories.

Aerial victories officially credited to Witold Urbanowicz:

Date		Victories	PAF Aircraft	Aircraft No.	Squadron No.
11 August 1940	1	Me 109-destroyed	Hurricane I	P3391	145
12 August 1940	1	Ju 88-destroyed	Hurricane I	R4177	
6 September 1940	1	Me 109 - destroyed	Hurricane I	V7242 RF-B	303
7 September 1940	1	Do 215 - destroyed	Hurricane I	R2685 RF-G	
	1	Me 109 - probable destroyed			
15 September 1940	2	Do 215 - destroyed	Hurricane I	V6684 RF-F	
26 September 1940	1	He 111 - destroyed	Hurricane I	P3901 RF-E	
27 September 1940	1	Do 17 - destroyed	Hurricane I	P3901 RF-E	
	1	Me 109 - destroyed			
	2	Ju 88 - destroyed			
30 September 1940	3	Me 109 - destroyed	Hurricane I	P3901 RF-E	
	1	Do 215 - destroyed			
11 December 1943	2	Ki-44 - destroyed	P-40K-1	—	75 FS

TOTAL: 17 destroyed, 1 probable destroyed.

On 20 October 1940 he was posted to HQ No. 11 Fighter Group as the Polish Liaison Officer. From 15 April until 27 May 1941 Urbanowicz organised and served as the first commander of the 1st Polish Fighter Wing at Northolt, West London.

In June 1941 he left for North America, to work in the Polish Mission in Canada (encouraging Americans of Polish parentage to join the Polish Air Force), but he also lectured on fighter tactics in the United States. He returned to Britain in mid-1942 and on 27 July 1942 he was posted for an instructor's course at No. 2 Flying Instructors' School at Montrose in Scotland, and then to No. 16 (Polish) SFTS as an instructor.

On 3 November 1942 Urbanowicz was appointed deputy air attaché at the Polish Embassy in Washington, D.C. In September 1943 he left the post at his own request after he was invited by General Chennault to fly at the Chinese-Japanese front. Between 23 October and 15 December 1943 Urbanowicz flew combat missions with the 16th Fighter Squadron USAAF based at Chengkung, 74th Fighter Squadron USAAF at Kunming, and the 75th Fighter Squadron USAAF at Hengyang.

In early 1944, Urbanowicz returned to Britain via the Middle East and was posted for staff duties. By August 1944 he was in Washington, D.C. again, as air attaché at the Polish Embassy. He remained at this post until July 1945, returning to Britain after the Allies withdrew recognition of the Polish government-in-exile.

Urbanowicz visited Poland in 1947, but the experience of communist rule discouraged him from re-settling in Poland. Instead, he emigrated to the United States, where he subsequently worked in the aircraft industry. His war-time experiences inspired him to write several books, including *Myśliwcy (Fighters)*, *Ogień nad Chinami (Fire over China)*, *Początek jutra (Beginning of Tomorrow)*, and *Świt zwycięstwa (Dawn of Victory)*.

In 1995, following the fall of communism in Poland, Urbanowicz was promoted to General of the Polish Air Force. In May 1996 he visited 1 Pułk Lotnictwa Myśliwskiego

'Warszawa' (1st Fighter Regiment 'City of Warsaw') on the 75th anniversary of the original 1 Pułk Lotniczy in Warsaw with which he had served before the war. Having finally come 'home' after fifty years, Urbanowicz gave his blessing to the young Polish fighter pilots in a heart-warming ceremony. He then returned to the United States, dying a few months later on 25 August 1996. He is buried in Doylestown, Pennsylvania.

Urbanowicz was awarded the Silver Cross of the Virtuti Militari, the Cross of Valour and three bars, and the British DFC. His biography by Wojciech Krajewski was published in 2008 in Polish under the title *Witold Urbanowicz— legenda polskich skrzydeł* (*Witold Urbanowicz—A Legend of Polish Wings*).

18 May 1996—Urbanowicz gives his blessing
to the young fighter pilots of
1 Pułk Lotnictwa Myśliwskiego 'Warszawa.'

Stefan Wójtowicz

Born on 19 June 1919 at Wypnicha in the Lublin region. In 1936 Wójtowicz joined the SPLdM, graduating as a fighter pilot in 1939. On 1 July 1939 he was posted to 111 Eskadra Myśliwska of 1 Pułk Lotniczy in Warsaw, with which he fought in September 1939.

On 18 September 1939 Wójtowicz crossed the Romanian border with his unit, eventually reaching France, where in 1940 he was posted to the section of Major Krasnodębski. He was then re-posted to that of Captain Kuzian, defending Nantes. After the fall of France he was evacuated to Britain.

On 2 August 1940 Wójtowicz was posted to No. 303 Squadron at Northolt, West London, as one of its initial group of pilots. On 3 September 1940 his Hurricane I no. R2688 RF-F was damaged in combat with a German fighter. He force-landed near Woodchurch, Kent, slightly wounded.

A week later, on 11 September 1940, at 16:25 hrs. Wójtowicz was shot down and killed while engaged in single-handed combat against several German fighters. His Hurricane I no. V7242 RF-B crashed in the limestone excavation at Westerham, Kent. He is buried at Northwood Cemetery, Middlesex, grave no. H 209.

Aerial victories officially credited to Stefan Wójtowicz:

Date		Victories	PAF Aircraft	Aircraft No.	Squadron No.
7 September 1940	2	Do 215 - destroyed	Hurricane I	P3939 RF-H	
11 September 1940	1	Me 110 - destroyed	Hurricane I	V7242 RF-B	303
	1	Me 110 - probable destroyed			

TOTAL: 3 destroyed, 1 probable destroyed.

Funeral of an officer and an NCO from No. 303 Squadron
(either Cebrzyński and Wójtowicz, who were both killed
in action on 11 September 1940, or Paszkiewicz and Andruszków,
who were both killed in action on 27 September 1940).

Kazimierz Wünsche

Born on 5 June 1919 at Jarosław. In 1936 Wünsche joined the SPLdM at Bydgoszcz, and graduated as a fighter pilot in 1939 at Krosno. He was posted to 111 Eskadra Myśliwska of 1 Pułk Lotniczy in Warsaw. He fought in September 1939 in 111 Eskadra within Brygada Pościgowa.

Wünsche crossed the Romanian border with his unit. From Romania he reached France by sea, arriving on 11 November 1939. He fought in France in the section of Lieutenant Ludwik Paszkiewicz attached to GC II/8. After the fall of France he was evacuated to Britain.

On 2 August 1940, Wünsche was posted to No. 303 Squadron as one of its initial group of pilots. On 9 September 1940 he was shot down in air combat against Messerschmitt 109s. Wounded and burnt, he baled out of his Hurricane I no. P3700 RF-E.

After nearly a month in hospital, Wünsche returned to fly with No. 303 Squadron until posted to No. 58 OTU as a flying instructor on 4 September 1942. On 1 January 1943 he was commissioned to the rank of Second Lieutenant. On 21 March 1943 he returned to No. 303 Squadron, and was posted for an officer's course at RAF Cosford, Shropshire. After the course he once again returned to No. 303 Squadron.

Aerial victories officially credited to Kazimierz Wünsche:

Date		Victories	PAF Aircraft	Aircraft No.	Squadron No.
31 August 1940	1	Me 109 - destroyed	Hurricane I	V7244 RF-C	
5 September	1	Me 109 - destroyed	Hurricane I	V7289 RF-S	
6 September	1	Me 109 - destroyed	Hurricane I	V7289 RF-S	303
	1	Me 109 - probable destroyed			
23 June 1941	1	Me 109 - destroyed	Spitfire II	P8325 RF-B	
3 July 1942	1/2	Ju 88 - destroyed	Spitfire VB	AB151 RF-F	

TOTAL: 4 destroyed, 1 shared destroyed, 1 probable destroyed.

On 11 October 1943 Wünsche transferred to the Polish Air Force Depot at Blackpool, Lancashire. From 18 April 1944 he resumed combat flying, this time with No. 315 Squadron, serving with it until late October. After a month's break, on 6 December 1944 he was appointed 'B' Flight commander in that squadron. His last assignment, on 6 December 1945, was as Navigation Officer in No. 309 Squadron.

Wünsche returned to Poland in 1947. He was accepted into the post-war Polish Air Force and flew as an instructor at the Oficerska Szkoła Lotnicza (Officers' Air School) at Dęblin. In 1952 he was expelled from the service for political reasons, and was subsequently persecuted by the communist regime then in power. After political conditions became somewhat liberalised in 1957, Wünsche joined the civilian air medical service that was being formed, and he also flew in the civilian air-sea rescue service. Wünsche lived in Warsaw. He died on 10 July 1980, and is buried at Powązki Cemetery in Warsaw.

Wünsche was awarded the Silver Cross of the Virtuti Militari, the Cross of Valour and three bars, the British DFM, and the British DFC. After the war he was awarded the Knight's Cross of the Order of Polonia Restituta for his work in the air medical service.

Distinguished Flying Cross

Jan Zumbach

Born on 14 April 1915 in Warsaw, Zumbach inherited Swiss citizenship from his father. In 1936 he joined the SPL (not disclosing his Swiss citizenship). He was commissioned in 1938 as a fighter pilot, and posted to 111 Eskadra Myśliwska of 1 Pułk Lotniczy in Warsaw. In May 1939 Zumbach was seriously injured in a flying accident.

Returning to operational flying at the beginning of September 1939, he did not participate in the fighting over Poland, but acted as a liaison pilot for bomber units. On 17 September Zumbach crossed the Romanian border with other Polish airmen, and arrived in France by sea on 30 October 1939.

During the Battle of France he flew in a Polish fighter section operating at Villacoublay and Clermont-Ferrand. Following the French collapse, he was evacuated to Britain in June 1940. Zumbach was posted to No. 303 Squadron on 2 August 1940 as one of its original group of pilots.

Although he survived the Battle of Britain unscathed (and with many victories to his credit), Zumbach very nearly lost his life on 9 May 1941 when he was shot down over the English Channel in Spitfire II P7962 RF-A. He baled out near Dover, Kent, with a wound to the head. On 13 October 1941 he was slightly wounded in combat over France.

Aerial victories officially credited to Jan Zumbach:

Date		Victories	PAF Aircraft	Aircraft No.	Squadron No.
7 September 1940	2	Do 215 - destroyed	Hurricane I	V7242 RF-B	303
9 September 1940	1	Me 109 - destroyed	Hurricane I	R2685 RF-G	
	1	Me 109 - probable destroyed			
11 September 1940	1	Me 109 - destroyed	Hurricane I	R2685 RF-G	
15 September 1940	1	Me 109 - destroyed	Hurricane I	P3577 RF-E	
26 September 1940	1	Me 109 - destroyed	Hurricane I	V6684 RF-F	
	1	He 111 - destroyed			
27 September 1940	1	Me 109 - destroyed	Hurricane I	V6684 RF-F	
2 July 1941	1	Me 109 - destroyed	Spitfire II	P8385 RF-A	
	1	Me 109 - probable destroyed			
13 October 1941	1	Me 109 - destroyed	Spitfire VB	AB976 RF-D	
	1	Fw 190 - damaged			
24 October 1941	1	Me 109 - destroyed	Spitfire VB	AB976 RF-D	
27 April 1942	1	Fw 190 - probable destroyed	Spitfire VB	BM144 RF-D	
19 August 1942	1	Fw 190 - destroyed	Spitfire VB	EP594 RF-D	
	1	Fw 190 - probable destroyed			
	1/3	He 111 - destroyed			
25 September 1944	1	Fw 190 - probable destroyed	Mustang III	HB866 JZ	133 Wing

TOTAL: 12 destroyed, 1 shared destroyed, 5 probable destroyed, 1 damaged.

In December 1941 Zumbach was posted to No. 58 OTU at Grangemouth in Scotland as an instructor. On 23 March 1942 he returned to No. 303 Squadron, becoming 'A' Flight commander. Two months later, on 19 May 1942, he was given command of No. 303 Squadron, a position he held until 1 December 1942. He was subsequently appointed Polish Liaison Officer to HQ No. 9 Group RAF. From April 1943 until the end of that year he studied at the Polish Air Force Staff College.

On 1 February 1944 Zumbach was appointed to command the 3rd Polish Wing. On 14 June 1944 he was re-posted to the HQ of No. 18 (Polish) Sector. On 8 July he was appointed to lead No. 135 Wing RAF which included No. 222 (British), No. 485 (New Zealand) and No. 349 (Belgian) Squadrons, but no Polish units. He thus had the distinction of being the only Polish officer to command a non-Polish fighter wing with the RAF. However, he remained at this post for only about a week, as a major reorganisation of the 2nd Tactical Air Force took place in mid-July 1944, and Zumbach took over No. 133 (Polish) Wing.

From January 1945 until October 1946 he was Operations Officer at No. 84 Group RAF on the liberated Continent. During an inspection flight in an unarmed aeroplane on 7 April 1945, he mistakenly landed in enemy-held territory, becoming a POW for the last month of World War II. Upon his return to Britain, Zumbach held non-flying postings within the Polish Air Force, but did some flying with No. 303 Squadron which was at that time commanded by his old squadron mate, Witold Łokuciewski.

After demobilisation Zumbach resumed his Swiss passport but stayed in Britain. He established a private enterprise, ostensibly for 'air transport' but in fact for smuggling. In the mid-1950s he opened a nightclub in Paris, and subsequently became a mercenary pilot during African wars in Congo and Biafra.

He wrote a book published in French as *Mister Brown* and then in English as *On Wings of War* which is often regarded as his memoirs, but is believed by some to be partly fiction.

Zumbach died on 3 January 1986 in France. In light of his adventurous post-war life, it is not surprising that his death was rumoured to be not due to natural causes. He is buried in the Polish Air Force section of the Powązki Cemetery in Warsaw.

Zumbach was awarded the Silver Cross of the Virtuti Militari, the Cross of Valour and three bars, and the British DFC.

Cross of Valour and three bars

303 SQUADRON
CLAIMED VICTORIES
DURING THE BATTLE OF BRITAIN

303 SQUADRON

CLAIMED VICTORIES

DURING THE BATTLE OF BRITAIN

Pilot	Claimed Victories			Combat Location
	Destroyed	Probable Destroyed	Damaged	
30 AUGUST 1940				
Paszkiewicz	Do 215 [1]	—	—	St. Albans
31 AUGUST 1940				
Ferić	Me 109	—	—	Biggin Hill
Henneberg	Me 109	—	—	
Karubin	Me 109	—	—	
Kellett	Me 109	—	—	
Szaposznikow	Me 109	—	—	
Wünsche	Me 109	—	—	
2 SEPTEMBER 1940				
Ferić	—	Me 109	—	English Channel
František	Me 109	—	—	—
Henneberg	—	—	Me 109	French coast
Rogowski	Me 109	—	—	
3 SEPTEMBER 1940				
František	He 113 [2]	—	—	Dover
5 SEPTEMBER 1940				
Forbes	Ju 88	—	—	Thames Haven
František	Ju 88 Me 109	—	—	
Karubin	Me 109 Me 109	—	—	
Kellett	Me 109	Me 109	—	
Łapkowski	Ju 88	—	—	
Wünsche	Me 109	—	—	

Continued

[1] Claimed as 'Do 215' but was in fact Messerschmitt Bf 110C W.Nr.3615 M8+MM of 4./ZG76, which crashed at Barley Beans Farm, Kimpton, Hertfordshire.

[2] Claimed by František and credited by RAF authorities as 'He 113,' but no such Heinkel type was actually in use during the Battle of Britain. The actual aircraft destroyed has not been positively identified.

Pilot	Claimed Victories			Combat Location
	Destroyed	Probable Destroyed	Damaged	
6 SEPTEMBER 1940				
Ferić	Me 109	—	—	Sevenoaks
Forbes	Me 109	Me 109	—	
František	Me 109	—	—	
Karubin	He 111	—	—	
Kellett	Do 215	—	—	
Urbanowicz	Me 109	—	—	
Wünsche	Me 109	Me 109	—	
7 SEPTEMBER 1940				
Daszewski	Do 215	Do 215	—	Essex
Forbes	Do 215	—	—	
Henneberg	Me 109	Me 109	—	
Łokuciewski	Do 215	Do 215	—	
Paszkiewicz	Do 215 Do 215	—	—	
Pisarek	Me 109	—	—	
Szaposznikow	Do 215 Me 109	—	—	
Urbanowicz	Do 215	Me 109	—	
Wójtowicz	Do 215 Do 215	—	—	
Zumbach	Do 215 Do 215	—	—	
9 SEPTEMBER 1940				
František	Me 109 He 111	—	—	Horsham
Kent	Me 110	Ju 88	—	— Beachy Head
Zumbach	Me 109	Me 109	—	
11 SEPTEMBER 1940				
Brzezowski	He 111 He 111	—	—	Horsham
Forbes	Do 215 Do 215	—	—	
František	Me 109 Me 109 He 111	—	—	
Henneberg	Me 109 He 111	—	—	

Continued

292

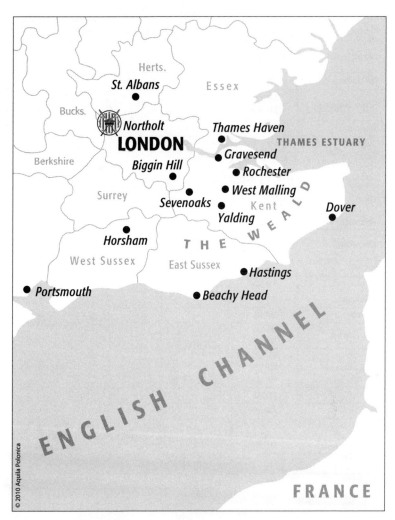

SOUTH-EAST ENGLAND AND CHANNEL COAST

Pilot	Claimed Victories			Combat Location
	Destroyed	Probable Destroyed	Damaged	
Continued	**11 SEPTEMBER 1940**			
Łokuciewski	Do 215 Me 109	—	—	Horsham
Paszkiewicz	Me 110	—	—	
Szaposznikow	Me 110 Me 110	—	—	
Wójtowicz	Me 110	Me 110	—	
Zumbach	Me 109	—	—	
	15 SEPTEMBER 1940			
Andruszków	Do 215 - shared	—	—	South-East London
Ferić	Me 109 Me 110	—	—	
František	Me 110	—	—	
Henneberg	Me 109 Do 215	—	—	
Kellett	Me 110	Do 215	—	
Łokuciewski	Me 109	—	—	
Paszkiewicz	Me 109	—	—	—
Pisarek	Me 109	—	—	Gravesend
Urbanowicz	Do 215 Do 215	—	—	
Wojciechowski	Do 215 - shared Me 109 Me 109	—	—	
Żak	Do 215	—	—	
Zumbach	Me 109	—	—	
	17 SEPTEMBER 1940			
Wojciechowski	Me 109	—	—	Thames Estuary
	18 SEPTEMBER 1940			
František	Me 109	—	—	West Malling
Jointly by 8 pilots	Do 215	—	—	Yalding
	23 SEPTEMBER 1940			
Kent	Me 109	—	FW 58	English Channel
Szaposznikow	Me 109	—	—	
	26 SEPTEMBER 1940			
Andruszków	Do 215	—	—	Portsmouth
Bełc	Me 109	—	—	
Forbes	He 111	—	—	

Continued

APPENDIX 5

Pilot	Claimed Victories			Combat Location
	Destroyed	Probable Destroyed	Damaged	
Continued	**26 SEPTEMBER 1940**			
František	He 111 He 111	—	—	Portsmouth
Grzeszczak	He 111	—	—	
Kellett	Me 109	—	—	
Kowalski	Me 109	—	—	
Paszkiewicz	He 111	—	—	
Urbanowicz	He 111	—	—	
Żak	He 111	—	He 111	
Zumbach	Me 109 He 111	—	—	
	27 SEPTEMBER 1940			
Ferić	Me 109 He 111	—	—	Horsham
Forbes	He 111	—	—	
František	He 111 Me 110	—	—	
Grzeszczak	Me 109	—	—	—
Henneberg	Me 109	—	—	
Kent	Ju 88	—	—	South-East London
Kowalski	—	—	He 111	
Szaposznikow	Me 109	—	—	—
Urbanowicz	Do 17 Me 109 Ju 88 Ju 88	—	—	Hastings
Żak	He 111	—	—	
Zumbach	Me 109	—	—	
	30 SEPTEMBER 1940			
František	Me 109	Me 109	—	South-East London
Karubin	Me 109	—	—	
Radomski	Do 215 - shared	—	—	
Urbanowicz	Me 109 Me 109 Do 215 Me 109	—	—	— English Channel

Continued

295

Pilot	Claimed Victories			Combat Location
	Destroyed	Probable Destroyed	Damaged	
1 OCTOBER 1940				
Kent	Me 109	Me 109	—	South Coast
5 OCTOBER 1940				
Bełc	Me 110	—	—	Rochester
Ferić	Me 110	—	—	
Henneberg	Me 110	—	—	
Karubin	Me 109	—	—	
Kellett	—	—	Me 109	
Palak	Me 109	—	Me 110	—
Pisarek	Me 110	—	Me 110	
Siudak	Me 109 Me 109 Me 110 - shared	—	Me 110	English Channel
7 OCTOBER 1940				
Bełc	Me 109	—	—	South London
Pisarek	Me 109	—	—	
Szaposznikow	Me 109	—	Me 109	

'Misia' the 303 Squadron mascot.

APPENDIX 6

BROTHERS IN ARMS:
THE 303 SQUADRON BADGE
AND THE
ORIGINAL KOŚCIUSZKO SQUADRON

APPENDIX 6

BROTHERS IN ARMS:
THE 303 SQUADRON BADGE
AND THE ORIGINAL KOŚCIUSZKO SQUADRON

Each unit in the Polish Air Force during World War II had its own badge, which was applied to both aircraft and uniforms. One of the most unique was that of No. 303 'Kościuszko' Squadron—a badge of rich historical tradition that honoured a shared heritage of independence with the United States of America, and the willingness to fight to protect that independence.

The Original Kościuszko Squadron

The original Kościuszko Squadron was a band of intrepid American World War I military pilots who volunteered to fly with the fledgling Polish Air Force in the Polish–Bolshevik War of 1919–1920.

At the end of World War I, Poland had finally regained its independence as a nation after 123 years of having been divided up by Austria, Prussia and Russia. But the new border between Poland and Russia had not been settled. The Polish leader, Józef Piłsudski, wanted to incorporate as much as possible of historic Poland's eastern territory. Vladimir Lenin, leader of Bolshevik Russia, wanted to reincorporate Poland into Russia and spread the communist revolution to western Europe—for the Bolsheviks, the shortest route to Berlin and Paris lay through Warsaw.

The Polish–Bolshevik War of 1919–1920 began almost immediately after the Armistice in World War I. Over a two-year period the newly independent Poland fought and defeated Bolshevik Russia.

Merian Cooper, an American pilot who had flown in the U.S. Army Air Service during World War I, recruited a small group of American military pilots as volunteers to help the Poles in their fight against Bolshevik Russia. He felt a debt of honour to Poland because of the assistance that two famous Polish generals, Kazimierz Pułaski and Tadeusz Kościuszko, had given to the nascent United States during the American Revolution—magnified by a family connection: Pułaski had fought and died at the side of Cooper's great-great-grandfather Colonel John Cooper during the Revolution. Cooper had been raised on tales of Poland's heroic but tragic history as recounted by Pułaski to Colonel Cooper and passed down through the Cooper family over the generations.

Cooper had hoped to recruit enough American pilots for two squadrons. But there were only enough volunteers to form one squadron, which eventually became the 7th 'Kościuszko' Squadron of the Polish Air Service, named in honour of General Tadeusz Kościuszko. The squadron was comprised of sixteen Americans, one Canadian and four Polish pilots, together with an all-Polish ground crew. Its initial American commander was Cedric Fauntleroy, an experienced World War I pilot who had served on the Western Front. When Fauntleroy was promoted to command a group of squadrons within the Polish Air Service, Cooper took over command of the 7th 'Kościuszko' Squadron.

The American pilots were based in a specially designed railway train that contained their headquarters, repair shops and bunks, and provided the mobility that the Polish campaigns demanded. They received the same pay and rank as their Polish counterparts. For their squadron badge,

Ludomił Rayski (*on the left*), future commander of the Polish Air Force, was the Polish commander of the unit which was eventually re-named the 7th 'Kościuszko' Squadron. Cedric Fauntleroy (*on the right*) was the initial American commander of the 7th 'Kościuszko' Squadron.

Naczelnik Państwa i Naczelny Wódz Józef Piłsudski dekoruje orde-
rem Virtuti Militari płk. Faunt-le-Roy'a.
The Chief of the State and Commander in Chief Józef Piłsudski
decorating Col. Faunt-le-Roy with the Virtuti Militari.

In recognition of their courage and their devotion to Poland's independence, nine American airmen were awarded Poland's highest military decoration, the Virtuti Militari.

In a graveside ceremony in Lwów, pilots of 111 Eskadra Myśliwska 'Kościuszko' honour the three American airmen of the original Kościuszko Squadron who lost their lives during the Polish–Bolshevik War.

The Ansaldo A.1 Balilla fighter '1' of the 7th 'Kościuszko' Squadron stationed at Mokotów shortly after the Polish–Bolshevik War.

During the German invasion of Poland in September 1939, 111 Eskadra Myśliwska 'Kościuszko,' equipped with P. 11 fighters, fought valiantly as part of the Brygada Pościgowa defending Warsaw.

A No. 303 Squadron Spitfire funded by the Municipal Borough of Hendon in north-west London. Sitting in the cockpit is RAF pilot T. B. Sim, who served with No. 303 Squadron for a brief period.

At the beginning of 1941, No. 303 Squadron was visited by Merian Cooper (*fourth from left*), founder and a commander of the original Kościuszko Squadron.

American pilot Elliott Chess created a design that combined both American and Polish traditions.

The Kościuszko Squadron fought with the Poles throughout virtually the entire Polish–Bolshevik War, flying several hundred missions. The Americans brought with them a potent combination of training, skill and experience. So effective were the squadron's low-altitude, machine-gun strafing runs that the Soviet Commissars placed a bounty of 12,500 gold rubles on each American pilot's head, and later doubled it. Each Kościuszko Squadron pilot carried a vial of potassium cyanide with him in case of capture.

Merian Cooper was a special case: the Bolsheviks had reportedly offered a bounty of half a million rubles for his capture. When Cooper was shot down behind enemy lines, he didn't dare admit his true identity. Instead, he was able to convince his captors that he was a mere enlisted man, showing them his hands, calloused and blistered from maintaining engines. After a year, he managed to escape from a prison camp near Moscow to safety in Latvia. Three other Americans were not so lucky: Edmund P. Graves, Arthur Kelly and T. V. McCallum lost their lives and are buried in Lwów (Graves died in a flying accident while on review for Marshal Piłsudski; Kelly and McCallum were killed in action).

Cooper, Fauntleroy and seven other American pilots of that original Kościuszko Squadron were awarded Poland's highest military decoration, the Virtuti Militari.

The tradition of the Kościuszko Squadron continued after the Americans returned home in 1921. One of the Warsaw-based fighter squadrons of the Polish Air Force, the 111 Eskadra Myśliwska (111th Fighter Flight) of the 1 Pułk Lotniczy (1st Air Regiment), adopted the Kościuszko name and badge. Before World War II, each year a section of this squadron flew to Lwów to take part in a formal ceremony honouring the three American pilots who had given their life for Polish independence.

But perhaps the highest honour was bestowed on that small band of American pilots from World War I by a group of Polish fighter pilots during World War II—No. 303 'Kościuszko' Squadron, whose extraordinary aerial combat skills and steely determination helped save Great Britain from conquest by Nazi Germany during the most critical days of the Battle of Britain.

The 303 Squadron Badge

The 303 Squadron badge is circular in form, and was based on the badge designed by the original Kościuszko Squadron in 1919.

A distinctive four-cornered red cap of traditional Polish style is set against a field of red stripes on a white background, red and white being two colours contained in both the Polish and American flags. Behind the red cap is a pair of crossed scythes. Thirteen blue stars encircle the badge, representing the thirteen original American states.

The cap and scythes commemorate the Kościuszko Uprising of 1794: ten years after General Tadeusz Kościuszko returned to Poland from America, he led the Polish people, many armed only with scythes, in what was ultimately a failed attempt to liberate Poland from Russia and Prussia.

The badge was applied to No. 303 Squadron aircraft throughout World War II. During the more than six years of the unit's existence, a number of different stencils were used. Individual elements—the hat, scythe and stars—varied in form and size, but there was never any doubt that they depicted *the* 303 Squadron badge.

Below:

7th 'Kościuszko' Squadron honour badge of 1920.

Above:

Variants of the Kościuszko Squadron emblem have been stenciled onto aircraft fuselages from 1919 up to the present day.

111 Eskadra Myśliwska 'Kościuszko' honour badge award document dated 19 May 1935.

Dr. Zygmunt Wodecki's 303 Squadron
honour badge and award document.

The 303 Squadron honour badge is visible on the left breast pocket of Urbanowicz's uniform.

On 27 November 1946, Squadron Leader Łokuciewski, the last commanding officer of No. 303 Squadron, removes the Kościuszko emblem from a PD-coded Mustang, thus marking the official disbanding of the most famous Polish fighter squadron in Great Britain.

No. 303 Squadron veteran Ludwik Kraszewski (*on the left*) and Colonel Robert Ciernak, then commanding officer of 1 Eskadra Lotnictwa Taktycznego. In the background is Ciernak's MiG-29 fighter with the Kościuszko Squadron emblem on its fuselage.

In addition, the Polish Air Force authorised a squadron 'honour badge' to be worn on the upper left pocket of the uniform jacket. The honour badge for No. 303 Squadron was a full-colour enameled metal version of the 303 Squadron badge with the addition of the number '303' at the bottom, about 40 mm in diameter with a screw back. The honour badges were awarded only to the commanding officers of the squadron, to pilots who had made at least one operational sortie or who had served faultlessly with the unit for three months, and to ground crew members after six months of faultless service. These badges were individually numbered on the reverse and bestowed in a special ceremony.

In addition to their honour badges, pilots also wore distinctively coloured scarves that identified their squadron. In general, of course, all fighter pilots wore silk scarves to prevent irritation to their neck skin from having to be constantly on the lookout in all directions (the collar of the regulation shirt being rather stiff). The pilots of No. 303 Squadron wore bright scarlet scarves.

On 27 November 1946, Squadron Leader Witold Łokuciewski, the last commanding officer of No. 303 Squadron, removed the 303 Squadron badge from the side of a Mustang coded PD, marking the end of the existence of the most celebrated Polish fighter squadron of World War II.

Thus, it seemed that the famed tradition of the Kościuszko Squadron had finally died. But it had not!— although it took nearly half a century, until after the fall of the communist regime in post-war Poland, for the Kościuszko Squadron to rise again. In the spring of 1996, a group of veterans of No. 303 Squadron led by Witold Urbanowicz, the legendary commander of the unit during the Battle of Britain, formally handed the unit's traditions to 1 Eskadra Lotnictwa

Myśliwskiego (1st Fighter Squadron) of the then 1 Pułk
Lotnictwa Myśliwskiego 'Warszawa' (1st Fighter Regiment
'City of Warsaw').

Three years later, in the spring of 1999, six pilots of the
1 Eskadra Lotnictwa Myśliwskiego based at Mińsk Mazowiecki
became the first Polish component of the united NATO
forces when Poland joined the Treaty. Now after subsequent
reorganisations, 1 Eskadra Lotnictwa Taktycznego (1st Tactical
Squadron) is based at 23 Baza Lotnicza (23rd Air Base) at Mińsk
Mazowiecki. The MiG aircraft of today's squadron display the
famous badge, as did the biplanes of American volunteers
defending Poland ninety years ago and the Hurricanes of
No. 303 Squadron defending London in 1940.

APPENDIX 7

THE SONG OF
303 SQUADRON

Preceding page—from the left:

Daszewski, Kustrzyński (*in the background*),
Kołaczkowski, Urbanowicz, Arentowicz
and Radomski.

THE SONG OF 303 SQUADRON

303 SQUADRON

by Czesław 'Czechura' Kałkusiński

An eagle in flight as the engines play a march
>In a grim dance with death, longing drives us.
>The roar of engines is the airman's own song,
>The roar of engines like our hearts resonates within us.

>>Through murk and thick fog,
>>In defence of foreign isles—
>>That's us, 303 Squadron,
>>That's us!

On our wings shine Polish emblems,
On our wings sing the winds of liberty,
Like a tune of the free—we sail over the earth,
To pound into dust that bed of crime and evil.

>>The propellers too play a melody of the heart.
>>This tune to battle calls us like a gust of vengeance.
>>That song, that's our song,
>>It plays to us on those emblems and on those wings,
>>A call to battle, a call to battle,
>>A soaring flight! A tune of victory.

Through murk and thick fog,
In defence of foreign isles—
That's us, 303 Squadron,
That's us!

Zbigniew Zieliński, former Polish Secretary of State for Veterans Affairs, was a teenaged forest partisan in the underground Armia Krajowa ('AK' or Home Army) stationed near Częstochowa during the war years. He recalls the circumstances under which the famous war-time song '303 Squadron' was written by one of the soldiers in his unit, pre-war poet Czesław Kałkusiński, whose nom de guerre[1] was 'Czechura':

> Parachute drops of supplies and weapons, which originated in England and were announced over the radio from London using a special code, had not only a practical value for the 'partisan brotherhood' but also a psychological one. They were a sign that someone was thinking about us, someone was supporting us.
>
> One day there was a particularly memorable drop in the Gidle forestry district. The drop went well, and the partisans were able to collect all the canisters. In one of the canisters there was a book in addition to the weapons and ammunition. Everyone thought at first that it was instructions for the operation of the PIAT[2] anti-tank weapons.
>
> But it was a book called *Dywizjon 303* written by Arkady Fiedler and published in London. The lads kept grabbing it from one another; some of them read it out loud so that the others could hear.

---

[1] All members of the World War II Polish underground resistance, both civil and military, adopted noms de guerre or pseudonyms which they used instead of their own names, hiding their real identities to protect their families, friends and even their villages or neighbourhoods from reprisals by the hostile German forces that occupied Poland.

[2] The PIAT (Projector, Infantry, Anti-Tank) was a hand-held anti-tank weapon of British design. Translator's note.

Pride swelled in our hearts that faraway over England, France and Germany Polish squadrons were fighting 'for your freedom and ours.'[3] Czechura, who shared the pleasure at the Polish squadron's achievements, wrote a poem to which Garda (Henryk Fajt) composed the music. Thus was born the song '303 Squadron.'

In the forest bunkers near Gorgoń, Czechura posted this poem, together with the music, on the wall. One day two officers from the AK Kielce district came round on an inspection. They saw '303 Squadron' hanging on the wall and, with the permission of our CO Andrzej, they took it. The music and the words reached London, probably by courier. The song '303 Squadron' was subsequently heard by our airmen on London radio.

The Polish airmen gratefully accepted this 'gift' from their comrades-in-arms in occupied Poland. They liked the song, but no-one knew the names of the lyricist and the composer. The copy simply gave their noms de guerre 'Czechura' and 'Garda.'

Years after the war Air Commodore Stanisław Skalski and Group Captain Witold Łokuciewski, who had returned to Poland, began inquiring about the song's creators. When I learned of their inquiry, I contacted my cousin, Group Captain Tadeusz Nowierski, also a pilot and

---

[3] '*Za waszą wolność i naszą*' was a Polish revolutionary slogan dating back to 1831, and was widely used by the Poles to express to their World War II allies that the Poles were fighting 'for your freedom and ours.' Translator's note.

the former commander of an RAF wing, and informed him that I knew the lyricist personally, and that he was my friend Czesław 'Czechura' Kałkusiński. Shortly thereafter the three airmen came to Radomsko. The meeting between the airmen and Czechura was very warm. There was a great deal of hugging and story-telling. Czechura was moved and delighted. He told us that a copy of the song had been sent to London during the war, but he himself still had the original. Thus we were able to see it.

1944—AK partisans operating in the forests of the Kraków-Częstochowa Upland, where soldier-poet Czesław 'Czechura' Kałkusiński was stationed.

APPENDIX 8

AGAINST ALL ODDS:
THE CREATION OF
THE POLISH AIR FORCE COLOUR

APPENDIX 8

AGAINST ALL ODDS:

THE CREATION OF

THE POLISH AIR FORCE COLOUR[1]

The Polish Air Force, barely twenty years old at the outbreak of World War II,[2] had no Colour of its own before the war.

Following the Nazi German invasion and occupation of Poland in September 1939, most of the Polish Air Force was able to escape to France, to continue the fight against Nazi Germany. Captain Jan Hryniewicz thought it would boost morale to fly a Colour created in occupied Poland specifically for the Polish airmen fighting abroad. He arranged for people

---

[1] 'Colour' is the military term for an identifying flag or pennant and is the emblem that represents the 'soul' of a unit, especially its battle honours. The pride in the unit Colour was such that, if it was captured by the enemy, the unit would often be disbanded. For example, in order to prevent the Colour of the Polish 4th Armoured Battalion (4 Batalionu Pancernego) from falling into German hands following the surrender of Warsaw in September 1939, the unit's Colour was ceremoniously burned at Mokotów Field. The battalion's Colour was not officially reinstated until October 1967 by veterans of its successor regiment, which remained in Great Britain after World War II.

[2] For 123 years, from the late 18th century until the end of World War I, Poland did not exist as a country. Divided up by Austria, Prussia and Russia in the Partitions of 1772, 1793 and 1795, Poland was not re-united as an independent nation until after the Armistice of November 1918 and the signing of the Treaty of Versailles in 1919, which officially ended World War I.

Immediately after regaining its independence, the fledgling country had to defend itself against attack by Bolshevik Russia, which wanted to reincorporate Poland into Russia and spread the communist revolution to Western Europe. In fighting the Polish–Bolshevik War of 1919–1920, the new nation was required to overcome a severe handicap: it had no pre-existing armed forces. In an extraordinary feat, soldiers of Polish ancestry who had been born and raised as Austrian, German or Russian citizens—trained on different equipment, with different methods and in different languages, and some of whom, just a couple of years earlier, had been fighting World War I on different sides—quickly organised themselves into a new Polish army and air force. Over a two-year period, the Poles fought and defeated the Russians.

from his home district of Wilno to make one for the Polish Air Force.

But creation of the Polish Air Force Colour was difficult and dangerous. The Wilno area was occupied by hostile forces of the Soviet Union, which had invaded Poland from the east on 17 September 1939. Designs for the Colour, drawn by two air force cadet-officers, Kazimierz Karaszewski and Zbigniew Wojda, were smuggled from France into Soviet-occupied Wilno via Switzerland.

In Wilno, Zofia Wasilewska-Swidow, aided by Father Kazimierz Kucharski, organized the clandestine effort. Finding people willing to work on the project was easy. Locating the necessary materials in Wilno or nearby Lithuania was impossible. Only one place had the necessary damask fabric and silver and gold embroidery thread: Berlin.

Neutral diplomats in Wilno came to the rescue, secretly procuring the precious supplies from Berlin, and the work began. Producing the Colour required months of painstaking labour and skill. To avoid detection, the covert work was divided among several families and religious communities, some renowned for their centuries-long tradition of embroidery.

The Polish Air Force Colour is in the traditional military form of a red cross on a white background. A round medallion occupies the centre. An embroidered portrait of Wilno's patron saint, Our Lady of Ostra Brama, fills the medallion on one side of the Colour. Above it is the national White Eagle; below, the words 'Bóg, Honor, Ojczyzna' (God, Honour, Fatherland).

Because the Colour was to fly in France, on its reverse the medallion features St. Theresa of Lisieux. Above are the words 'Wilno 1940'; below, the statement 'Miłość Żąda Ofiary' (Love Demands Sacrifice). In the upper right-hand corner appears the red and white chessboard of the Polish Air Force; the other

16 July 1941—the official ceremony of handing the Colour over to the Polish Air Force at RAF Swinderby in Lincolnshire.

From the right: General Władysław Sikorski and Air Chief Marshal Sir Charles Portal take the salute.

29 March 1942—No. 303 Squadron pilot Daszewski hands the Polish Air Force
Colour to the commander of No. 304 Bomber Squadron.

4 September 1992—the ceremony of handing the Colour to the Polish Air Force
in Poland by representatives of the Polish Air Force Association in Britain.
The Colour party of the Polish Air Force and Air Defence marches past a
group of Polish Air Force veterans.

corners display flying badges and the crest of the Polish Air Force College at Dęblin.

The selection of a French saint for the reverse of the medallion proved premature. By the time the Colour was finished in June 1940, France had fallen to the Germans, and the Polish Air Force was escaping once again, this time to Great Britain.

The Colour was ready at last, but how could it be delivered to the Polish Air Force in Great Britain? Wilno was completely cut off from Western Europe by the Soviets.

Once again, after some abortive Polish attempts, a member of the neutral diplomatic corps came to the rescue—the Japanese consul in Lithuania arranged to smuggle the Colour out of Wilno, via Berlin, to neutral Stockholm in the diplomatic luggage of one of his couriers. From Stockholm, the Colour eventually reached London in March 1941.

Finally, on 16 July 1941, in a solemn ceremony at RAF Swinderby in Lincolnshire, the Colour was presented to the Polish Commander-in-Chief, General Sikorski, by General Żeligowski, himself from Wilno. General Sikorski in turn presented the new Colour to Air Vice-Marshal Ujejski, Commander-in-Chief of the Polish Air Force. In attendance were the President of the Polish government-in-exile Władysław Raczkiewicz and other dignitaries, all of whom hammered their names on silver nails into the flagstaff from which the Colour hung. The new Colour was then handed to No. 300 Bomber Squadron, the senior Polish Air Force squadron in England.

The people of occupied Wilno learned that their creation had finally been delivered by way of a BBC radio broadcast from London secretly monitored by Polish underground forces.

Thereafter during the war, the Colour was passed in rotation from squadron to squadron every three months—a source of pride and inspiration, and a symbol of unity between the Polish Air Force in exile and the beleaguered homeland. No. 303 Squadron took possession of the Colour from No. 302 Squadron at Northolt, West London on 20 January 1942 and passed it on to No. 304 Bomber Squadron at Northolt on 29 March 1942.

At the end of World War II, Poland was consigned to the Soviet sphere of influence by its Western allies. Consequently the Polish Air Force Colour, together with all the Colours of the Polish armed forces of the government-in-exile, was deposited for safekeeping at the General Sikorski Historical Institute in London until it could be returned to a free Poland. That did not happen until nearly fifty years later, following the overthrow of the Polish communist regime in 1989.

The Polish Air Force Colour was returned to Poland, the home of its creation, on 4 September 1992 in an historic ceremony at Piłsudski Square in Warsaw. The then president of the Polish Republic, Lech Wałęsa, accepted the Colour in the presence of several hundred members of the Polish Air Force Association who had gathered from around the world, numerous Polish government officials, military leaders and the general public, as well as several representatives of the Royal Air Force who had escorted the Colour by air from England.

APPENDIX 9

OPERATIONAL UNITS OF
THE POLISH AIR FORCE
IN GREAT BRITAIN
DURING WORLD WAR II

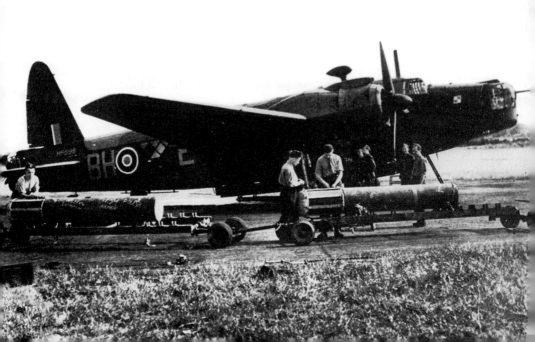

APPENDIX 9

OPERATIONAL UNITS OF
THE POLISH AIR FORCE IN GREAT BRITAIN
DURING WORLD WAR II

UNIT	ROLE	PERIOD		BASE	NOTES
No. 300 Squadron 'Masovian'[1]	Bomber	Jul. 1940	Dec. 1946	Britain	
No. 301 Squadron 'Pomeranian'	Bomber	Jul. 1940	Apr. 1943	Britain	
	Special Duties	Nov. 1944	Mar. 1945	Italy	Re-formed by expanding No. 1586 Flight
	Transport	Apr. 1945	Dec. 1946	Britain	
No. 302 Squadron 'City of Poznań'[2]	Day Fighter	Jul. 1940	Aug. 1944	Britain	Since autumn 1943 part of the 2nd Tactical Air Force
		Aug. 1944	Oct. 1946	Western Europe	
		Oct. 1946	Dec. 1946	Britain	
No. 303 Squadron 'City of Warsaw' /'Kościuszko'[3]	Day Fighter	Aug. 1940	Dec. 1946	Britain	
No. 304 Squadron 'Silesian'	Bomber	Aug. 1940	May 1942	Britain	
	Anti-Submarine	May 1942	Jul. 1945	Britain	
	Transport	Jul. 1945	Dec. 1946	Britain	
No. 305 Squadron 'Wielkopolska Province'	Bomber	Aug. 1940	Nov. 1944	Britain	Since autumn 1943 part of the 2nd Tactical Air Force
		Nov. 1944	Oct. 1946	Western Europe	
		Oct. 1946	Dec. 1946	Britain	
No. 306 Squadron 'City of Toruń'	Day Fighter	Aug. 1940	Dec. 1946	Britain	Autumn 1943 to summer 1944 part of the 2nd Tactical Air Force
No. 307 Squadron 'City of Lwów'	Night Fighter	Aug. 1940	Dec. 1946	Britain	

Continued

[1] Non-fighter units of the Polish Air Force were given names related to historical provinces of Poland.

[2] Fighter units (except No. 315) were given names related to major Polish cities.

[3] See Appendix 6 for a history of the original Kościuszko Squadron.

UNIT	ROLE	PERIOD		BASE	NOTES
No. 308 Squadron 'City of Kraków'	Day Fighter	Sept. 1940	Aug. 1944	Britain	Since autumn 1943 part of the 2nd Tactical Air Force
		Aug. 1944	Oct. 1946	Western Europe	
		Oct. 1946	Dec. 1946	Britain	
No. 309 Squadron 'Czerwieńska Province'	Army Co-operation	Oct. 1940	Feb. 1943	Britain	
	Fighter-Reconnaissance	Feb. 1943	Oct. 1944		
	Day Fighter	Oct. 1944	Dec. 1946		
No. 315 Squadron 'Dęblin'[4]	Day Fighter	January 1941	Dec. 1946	Britain	Autumn 1943 to summer 1944 part of the 2nd Tactical Air Force
No. 316 Squadron 'City of Warsaw'	Day Fighter	Feb. 1941	Dec. 1946	Britain	
No. 317 Squadron 'City of Wilno'	Day Fighter	Feb. 1941	Aug. 1944	Britain	Since autumn 1943 part of the 2nd Tactical Air Force
		Aug. 1944	Oct. 1946	Western Europe	
		Oct. 1946	Dec. 1946	Britain	
No. 318 Squadron 'City of Gdańsk'	Fighter-Reconnaissance	Apr. 1943	Aug. 1943	Britain	
		Sept. 1943	Apr. 1944	Middle East	
		May 1944	Aug. 1946	Italy	
		Aug. 1946	Dec. 1946	Britain	
No. 663 Squadron	Artillery Spotting	Sept. 1944	Oct. 1946	Italy	
'C' Flight, No. 138 Squadron RAF (also known as No. 301 Special Duties Flight)	Special Duties	Apr. 1943	Nov. 1943	Britain	Formed as an all-Polish flight by expanding the Polish section of No. 138 Squadron; re-formed into the independent No. 1586 Flight

Continued

---

[4] Unlike the other Polish Air Force fighter squadrons, No. 315 was named for the town of Dęblin, the seat of the Polish Air Force College from 1927 to date.

UNIT	ROLE	PERIOD		BASE	NOTES
No. 1586 Flight	Special Duties	Nov. 1943	Dec. 1943	North Africa	Formed by separating the Polish 'C' Flight from No. 138 Squadron RAF
		Dec. 1943	Nov. 1944	Italy	Expanded into No. 301 Squadron
'C' Flight, No. 145 Squadron RAF (also known as the 'Polish Combat Team' or the 'Polish Fighting Team')	Day Fighter	Mar. 1943	May 1943	North Africa	Dubbed 'Skalski's Circus' by the press

A de Havilland Mosquito fighter-bomber of No. 305 Squadron.

**WINNER of the GOLD Award
for HISTORY and the
SILVER Award for
INTERIOR DESIGN** at the
2011 Benjamin Franklin Awards

A Selection of the **HISTORY BOOK CLUB®** and
the **MILITARY BOOK CLUB®**

Excerpted in Smithsonian's Air & Space Magazine!

"Deserves five stars for every single one of its pages. Vivid and
thrilling almost beyond measure."
— *Waterstones Bookseller Review*

"About as exciting as it gets. The author actually puts the reader
in the cockpit as fighters climb and dive and twist and turn in
dogfights."
— *The Washington Times*

"Compelling."
— *Flying Magazine*

"Vividly captures the drama, the danger, and the spirit of the
times."
— *College & Research Libraries News*

"Wonderful account of the Poles' heroic deeds."
— **Lynne Olson and Stanley Cloud, authors of**
   A Question of Honor

"Superb. A riveting read."
— *Cosmopolitan Review*

"Does a terrific job bringing to life an extraordinary moment in
the history of the war. Exceptionally high quality."
— *Sarmatian Review*

"Captivating. Nothing will surpass Fiedler's text in this very attractive book from Aquila Polonica."
— *Stone & Stone, Second World War Books*

"A lively epic. Readers feel they're in those planes."
— *The Polish American Journal*

"A story of heroic pilots who know no fear."
— *Polish Review*

Also from Aquila Polonica Publishing...

Fighting Auschwitz: The Resistance Movement in the Concentration Camp
by Józef Garliński

- Hardcover: 978-1-60772-024-9 ($42.95)
  Trade Paperback: 978-1-60772-025-6 ($34.95)
- 575 pages. More than 200 photos, maps and illustrations. Includes five Appendices, extensive Bibliography and detailed Indexes.
- Nonfiction.

The incredible story of underground resistance among the prisoners at the infamous Auschwitz concentration camp, based on extensive unpublished as well as published first-person accounts and archival sources. Out of print for decades, this important book is now being released in a new second edition, with a new introduction by Professor Antony Polonsky. **"The definitive study of the topic."**
— **Prof. Antony Polonsky, Emeritus Professor of Holocaust Studies, Brandeis University, and Chief Historian, POLIN Museum of the History of Polish Jews**

The Auschwitz Volunteer: Beyond Bravery
by Captain Witold Pilecki
Translated by Jarek Garliński
Introduction by Norman Davies
Foreword by Rabbi Michael Schudrich, Chief Rabbi of Poland

- Hardcover: 978-1-60772-009-6 ($42.95)
  Trade Paperback: 978-1-60772-010-2 ($34.95)
  Ebook: 978-1-60772-014-0 ($19.99)
  Audiobook: Audible.com and Brilliance Audio
- 464 pages. More than 80 black and white photos, maps and illustrations; contextualizing historical material; four Appendices; Discussion Questions; Index.
- Nonfiction.
- A Featured Selection of the **History Book Club**; a Selection of the **Book-of-the-Month Club** and the **Military Book Club.**

- Winner of the 2012 PROSE Award for Biography & Autobiography.
- Winner of the 2013 Benjamin Franklin SILVER Award for Autobiography/
  Memoir.

In one of the most heroic acts of WWII, Pilecki volunteered for an almost certainly suicidal undercover mission: get himself arrested and sent to Auschwitz as a prisoner in order to smuggle out intelligence about the camp and build a resistance organization among the prisoners. His clandestine reports from Auschwitz were among the first to reach the Allies, beginning in early 1941. He accomplished his mission, barely surviving nearly three years before escaping. Pilecki's most comprehensive eyewitness report on his mission is published here in English for the first time.

"A historical document of the greatest importance."
— *The New York Times,* Editors' Choice

The Color of Courage—A Boy at War:
The World War II Diary of Julian Kulski

by Julian Kulski

Foreword by Lech Wałęsa, Nobel Peace Prize Laureate
Introduction by Rabbi Michael Schudrich, Chief
Rabbi of Poland

- Hardcover: 978-1-60772-015-7 ($29.95)
  Trade Paperback: 978-1-60772-016-4 ($19.95)

- 496 pages. More than 150 black and white photos,
  maps and illustrations; 11 groundbreaking Digital Extras;
  contextualizing historical material; two Appendices;

Discussion Questions; Index. Educators' Guide correlated to Common Core Standards, Grades 9–12, available free online.
- Nonfiction.
- A Selection of the **History Book Club** and the **Military Book Club.**
- Winner of 2015 Benjamin Franklin GOLD Award for Interior Design and
  SILVER for Autobiography/Memoir.
- Finalist, *Foreword Reviews* IndieFab BOOK OF THE YEAR Award.

This remarkable diary follows Kulski, a 10-year-old Boy Scout when WWII begins, as he is recruited into the clandestine Polish Underground Army by his Scoutmaster, undertakes a secret mission into the Warsaw Ghetto, is captured by the Gestapo, sentenced to Auschwitz, rescued, fights in the Warsaw Uprising and ends as a 16-year-old German POW, risking a dash for freedom onto an American truck instead of waiting for "liberation" by the Soviets.

"Absorbing, inspiring, and tragic." — *Publishers Weekly*

Echoes of Tattered Tongues: Memory Unfolded
by John Z. Guzlowski

- Hardcover: 978-1-60772-021-8 ($21.95)
- 200 pages. 6 black and white photos; Discussion Questions.
- Nonfiction.
- **Winner of 2017 MONTAIGNE MEDAL for Most Thought-Provoking Book.**
- **Winner of 2017 Benjamin Franklin GOLD Award for Poetry.**

In this major tour de force, Guzlowski traces the arc of one of the millions of immigrant families of America, in this case, survivors of the maelstrom of World War II. Through a haunting collage—poems, prose and prose poems, frozen moments of time, sometimes dreamlike and surreal, other times realistic and graphic—the story unfolds backwards through time. This is the story of Guzlowski's own family: his parents were taken as slave laborers by the Germans and barely survived; his sister and he were born in Displaced Persons camps. Raw and at the same time compassionate, Guzlowski illuminates a hidden facet of World War II and reflects the many ways in which trauma echoes through time, leaving us with a deeper, more visceral understanding of the human costs of war.
"Deeply moving. A powerful, lasting, and sometimes shocking book. Superb."
— **Kelly Cherry, Poet Laureate of Virginia (2010–2012)**

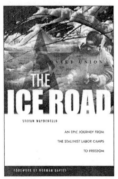

The Ice Road: An Epic Journey from the Stalinist Labor Camps to Freedom
by Stefan Waydenfeld
Foreword by Norman Davies

- Hardcover: 978-1-60772-002-7 ($28.95)
  Trade Paperback: 978-1-60772-003-4 ($18.95)
  Ebook: 978-1-60772-017-1 ($12.99)
  Audiobook: Audible.com
- 416 pages. More than 70 black and white photos, maps and illustrations; contextualizing historical material; author interview; Reading Group Guide.
- Nonfiction.

- A Selection of the **History Book Club** and the **Military Book Club**.
- **Winner of 2011 Benjamin Franklin SILVER Award for Autobiography/Memoir.**

Fourteen years old when WWII began, Stefan Waydenfeld and his family were deported by cattle car in 1940 from Poland to a forced labor camp in the frozen wastes of the Russian arctic north. Coming of age was never so dangerous—but

Waydenfeld recounts the experience with a teenager's irrepressible curiosity and subversive humor.

"Extraordinary." — Anne Applebaum, Pulitzer Prize-winning author of *Gulag*

Maps and Shadows: A Novel
by Krysia Jopek
- Hardcover: 978-1-60772-007-2 ($19.95)
  Trade Paperback: 978-1-60772-008-9 ($14.95)
  Ebook: 978-1-60772-013-3 ($9.99)
- 168 pages. Fleven black and white illustrations and map; Bibliography; Reading Group Guide.
- Fiction.
- **Winner of 2011 Benjamin Franklin SILVER Award for Historical Fiction.**

Stunning debut novel from poet Jopek illuminates a little known chapter of WWII—the Soviet deportations of 1.5 million Polish civilians to forced labor camps in Siberia. Told from the points of view of four members of one family, *Maps and Shadows* traces their journeys from Poland to Siberia, on divergent paths to Persia, Palestine and Italy, to Uzbekistan and Africa, converging in England and finally settling in the U.S. Fresh stylistic approach fuses minimalist narrative with lush lyricism.

"Jopek…shows how very talented she is." — *Nightreader*

The Mermaid and the Messerschmitt: War Through a Woman's Eyes, 1939-1940
by Rulka Langer
- Hardcover: 978-1-60772-000-3 ($29.95)
  Trade Paperback: 978-1-60772-001-0 ($19.95)
  Ebook: 978- 1-60772-018-8 ($12.99)
  Audiobook: Audible.com
- 496 pages. More than 100 black and white photos, maps and illustrations; contextualizing historical material; Reading Group Guide (included in paperback; online for hardcover).
- Nonfiction.
- A Selection of the **Book-of-the-Month Club,** the **History Book Club** and the **Military Book Club.**
- **Winner of 2010 Benjamin Franklin SILVER Award for Best First Book (Nonfiction).**

Thoroughly modern, Vassar-educated career woman Langer risked her life and relied on her wits to keep her two small children and elderly mother out of harm's way in Warsaw during the first six months of WWII. Engaging, clear-eyed chronicle sparkles. **"Absolutely one of the best." — Alan Furst, bestselling author of *The Foreign Correspondent* and *The Spies of Warsaw***

Siege: World War II Begins
Filmed and narrated by Julien Bryan
- DVD Video, all regions: 978-1-60772-006-5 ($14.95)
- Black and white newsreel, newly restored
  (10-minute run time); plus Special Features:
  26 color screens of text, still photos and maps; historic
  4-minute audio essay by Julien Bryan for
  Edward R. Murrow's 1950s radio show "This I Believe."

A "must have" for every WWII collection! First time available on DVD. This rare historic newsreel was among the first WWII film footage to come out of Europe. Renowned American photojournalist Julien Bryan's gut-wrenching images of the Siege of Warsaw in September 1939 shocked the American public into awareness of the devastation of modern warfare and the looming danger posed by Nazi Germany.

Nominated for an Oscar in 1940. **Inducted into the U.S. National Film Registry** in 2006 as one of the nation's most "culturally, historically or aesthetically significant films."

Author **ARKADY FIEDLER** (1894–1985) was born in Poznań, Poland, educated at the Jagiellonian University in Kraków, in Poznań and at the University of Leipzig.

A best-selling travel writer researching in Tahiti when World War II began, Fiedler made his way back to Europe and joined the Polish Army in France after Poland had fallen to the Germans. Fiedler managed to get to England with other Polish forces after the fall of France. He undertook to chronicle the extraordinary achievements of 303 Squadron during the Battle of Britain with the blessing of Polish Prime Minister and Commander-in-Chief General Władysław Sikorski.

Fiedler's thirty-two books have been translated into twenty-three languages, selling over 10 million copies. *303 Squadron* is his most famous and popular book.

Translator **JAREK GARLIŃSKI** was born in London, England, and grew up bilingual in English and Polish. His father was noted historian and author Józef Garliński, a former prisoner at Auschwitz-Birkenau. His mother Eileen Short-Garlińska was one of only a few Britons who spent World War II in Warsaw. Both parents served in the Polish Underground army during the war.

Educated at the University of Nottingham, the University of Grenoble, and the School of Slavonic and East European Studies at the University of London, Garliński is fluent in English, French, Polish and Russian, with a distinguished career in education. He has translated numerous books of Polish literature and history, specialising in the World War II era.